WANDERLIST BLUEPRINT

A practical guide to turning your travel dreams into a lifetime of unforgettable memories.

Jennifer Martin

Sharing the World Press

Wanderlist Blueprint

First edition, 2025

Published by Sharing the World Press
ISBN: 978-1-7643340-0-6

To my husband, Andy.
Thank you for always letting me hold the passports.

TABLE OF CONTENTS

AUTHOR'S NOTE

My passion for travel began with an unexpected invitation. It was a regular Thursday afternoon in 1997, and my boyfriend (now my husband, Andy) called me with a wild idea: *"American Airlines has round-trip flights to London for $150. Do you want to go for the weekend?"* We had barely any stamps in our passports and no real travel savvy. I had recently started a new job and therefore had no vacation days in sight, but hey, why not? I talked it over with my boss, promised to make up the time, and off we went. That impromptu trip kick-started our travels to more than 70 countries across all seven continents and sparked a spirit of exploration that eventually led us to move from the US to Australia.

The thrill of discovering new places, embracing diverse cultures, and enjoying unique experiences is an intrinsic part of who I am. I am driven by a restless curiosity to explore whenever time and resources allow. Photography shapes the core of my journeys, whether it is capturing the landscapes of the southwestern United States, trekking with gorillas in Uganda, or swimming with humpback whales in Tonga.

Here is the catch: I have always had a full-time job (and no one is paying me to pose in flowing dresses on cliff edges). I have made it my mission to squeeze the most adventure out of ordinary paychecks and annual leave. Travel keeps me sane at work and is the reward I provide myself for saving instead of splurging. Back in 1999, my first website was called "WhyWeWork," because that is exactly what Andy and I did. We worked so we could travel and photograph the world. Years later, someone bought the domain, which ended up funding a year of adventures.

I have always believed that travel is a privilege, but not a luxury reserved for the elite. It is an attainable dream for those who are willing to prioritize it and make a conscious effort to turn their Wanderlist into reality.

I also want to acknowledge that I write this from a place of deep gratitude and awareness. I know how fortunate I am in health, opportunity, and circumstance to have been able to travel the way I have. Not everyone is able to save easily, take time off work, or have the support systems that make travel possible.

What I hope to offer here is not a promise but a blueprint: a set of tools and strategies that can help you make progress, whatever your starting point or scale might be. I am at the far end of the spectrum; travel is a defining part of my identity, and sharing what I have learned is part of my purpose.

All those lessons, experiments, and discoveries are what eventually came together into the idea for this book. I wanted to share my knowledge, my experiences, and my secrets for making travel an integral part of your life, despite the constraints of time and finances. I have navigated the intricacies of maximizing annual leave, uncovered the magic of strategically timed trips, and devised ingenious ways to save for adventures, all while maintaining full-time jobs and everyday responsibilities.

By profession, I work in experience design and innovation. You will notice tools, frameworks, and approaches throughout this book that resonate with the systematic thinking I have honed in my career. Just as in my work, where I use design and methodologies to solve complex problems, this travel planning guide applies a structured approach to help you articulate and achieve your travel goals. I understand the value of data-driven decision-making, so you will notice practical tips on research and analysis to enhance your travel planning process.

So, join me on this adventure, where I will share practical advice, heartfelt stories, and the unwavering belief that travel is not just about the destination; it is about the journey, the experiences, and the memories that enrich our lives. Together, we will craft your ultimate travel adventure and show you how to make your Wanderlist dreams come true.

INTRODUCTION

Have you ever caught yourself scrolling flight deals or staring at a map, imagining where you would go if time and money were not in the way? That tug you feel is the magnet of travel. It pulls us toward the extraordinary, not the highlight reels shared online.

Think of what never makes it into the photo. Imagine the eerie chorus of howler monkeys at dawn in the Costa Rican rainforest. Taste the tartness of fresh calafate berries in Patagonia. Smell a pungent penguin colony long before you see the 250,000 birds behind it. Feel the sting of minus 20° air on your face while watching a polar bear nurse her cubs, or the sweat trickling down your back as you trek through the steamy Bornean rainforest for a glimpse of wild orangutans.

Those are the moments when travel sinks in. Travel leaves us with memories that outlast anything we could buy.

Some people measure wealth in dollars. I measure it in experience points. Every time you step into the unknown, push beyond your comfort zone, or say yes to an adventure you have dreamed about, you are adding to that account. A single trip can shake you out of routine, reframe your perspective, and give you stories you will carry forever.

This book is about helping you design a plan for the trips you will look back on forever, with practical steps, strategies, and a little inspiration along the way. By the end, you will not just have a list of destinations. You will have a plan for filling your life with experiences that make you feel truly alive.

Why "Wanderlist" Instead of "Bucket List"?

Before we embark on this journey together, I want to address the term I will be using throughout this book: "Wanderlist." You might be wondering why I chose this phrase over the more common "bucket list."

A "bucket list" suggests a checklist of things to do before you, well, "kick the bucket." I would rather think of travel as something richer than ticking boxes.

"Wanderlist," on the other hand, conjures an image of a grand, epic journey. It is an expedition into the unknown, a quest for the extraordinary, and a testament to the human spirit's boundless curiosity. It is about crafting a personal narrative of exploration and discovery, one that reflects your unique desires and aspirations. It is the art of wandering with intent, a conscious choice to chase experiences that excite you.

Throughout this book, I will guide you on how to define and achieve your Wanderlist, helping you transform your travel dreams into tangible, awe-inspiring experiences. So, let us ditch the checklist mentality, bring back the wonder, and map out an adventure that not only takes you places but also changes how you see the world and yourself.

How This Book Works

This is not just a book to read; it is a book to *use*. Each step comes with an activity designed to help you put ideas into practice right away. Do not skim past them. The insights only stick if you pause, grab a notebook, and try them for yourself.

The structure is simple but deliberate. The early steps are quick, light, and fun: jotting down sparks of inspiration, sketching a map of ideas, and thinking about what excites you. That is the easy part: making the list.

But the deeper you go, the more involved the work becomes. Turning daydreams into reality means planning around money, time, and priorities. It means making choices, building systems, and following through. These steps are longer because real travel planning takes more than inspiration; it takes intention.

So, if the first chapters feel like a breeze and the later ones feel like more work, that is by design. Start where you are, keep moving forward, and remember: every activity completed is a step closer to departing for your dream destination.

How Can a Wanderlist Help You Achieve Your Travel Goals?

A Wanderlist is more than just a collection of places you would like to visit; it is like a compass that steers you through the vast world of travel, a spark that ignites your wanderlust, and a blueprint for realizing your most cherished experiences. Here are four ways that a Wanderlist can assist you in reaching your travel aspirations.

1. **Stay Motivated and Focused**

   Your Wanderlist is your daily dose of inspiration. In the middle of work and life, it keeps your goals front and center. A photo of the Northern Lights, a screen capture of a lodge you want to visit, or even a picture of a beach can be enough to keep the dream alive until you book the trip.

2. **Plan Trips Effectively**

   Good travel planning takes more than wishful thinking. A Wanderlist helps you organize ideas, so you are in the right place at the right time. By grouping destinations by season, proximity, or theme, you can make smarter choices, avoid missed opportunities, and get the most from your time and money.

3. **Make the Most of Your Travels**

   Travel is an investment, and your Wanderlist helps you get the best return. It guides you toward experiences that match your passions, whether that means hiking in national parks, exploring street food markets, or diving into history (or the ocean). The result is travel that feels richer and more intentional than a standard vacation.

4. **Create Lasting Memories**

   The best souvenirs are not things you squeeze into a suitcase. They are the stories and memories you bring home and retell for years. Every entry on your Wanderlist is a chance to create one of those moments, something worth sharing, worth remembering, and worth carrying for a lifetime.

A Wanderlist is not just a wish list. It is a practical tool that keeps you motivated, helps you plan smarter, and ensures your trips are filled with meaningful experiences. Most of all, it turns daydreams into memories that become part of your life's story.

Wanderlist Journey

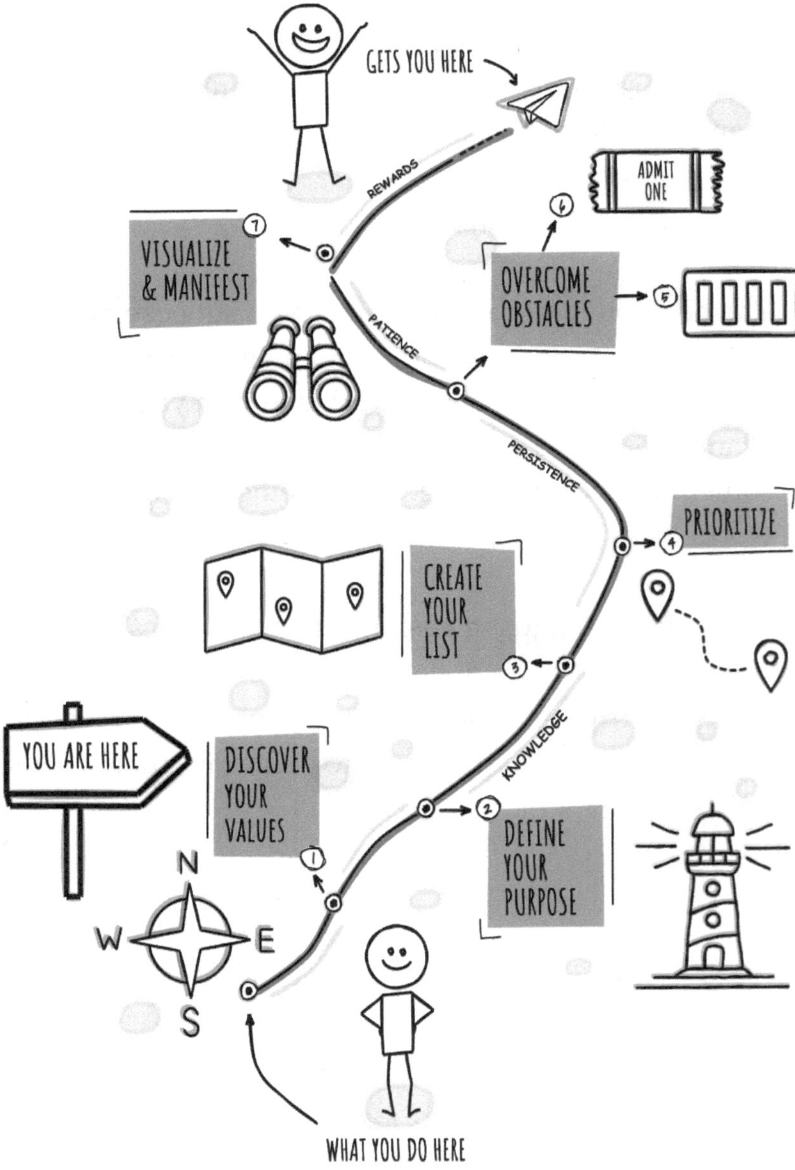

STEP 1

DISCOVERING YOUR TRAVEL VALUES

On the island of Nevis, I learned that a beach chair and endless downtime are not my idea of a wonderful trip. At first, it seemed perfect: quiet mornings, turquoise water, and no obligations. But after a few days, I was restless. I rented a car, drove inland, and went looking for the island's vervet monkeys. Photographing them was unexpectedly thrilling, and that small detour changed everything. I realized what I valued most in travel was not relaxation, but adventure, discovery, and wildlife encounters. That shift eventually led me to Costa Rica, the Galápagos, and eventually Africa, chasing animals with my camera instead of cocktails by the pool.

That is the power of knowing your travel values. Your travel values are more than just preferences; they act as a compass, guiding you towards trips that are meaningful, memorable, and deeply "you." Once you know what is important, it is easier to choose destinations, reject trips that do not fit, and prioritize the ones that do.

So, what do you value? Is it adventure, cultural immersion, food, nature, connection, or something else? Your values do not have to look like mine, and they will probably change over time. But getting clear on them now is the first step to building a Wanderlist that feels like a reflection of your true self.

Travel values come in many forms, and no two travelers are exactly alike. Some people crave the thrill of adventure, others find joy in slowing down, and many of us fall somewhere in between. Here are a few examples that may spark your thinking:

- **Adventure and Exploration**: pushing boundaries with new and thrilling experiences, from hiking remote trails to diving in wild waters. One of my favorite examples was the cross-island hike in the Cook Islands. We had not done any research, started from the wrong end, and hiked it backwards. It should have been frustrating, but instead it was exhilarating. That trip reminded me that adventure does not need to be perfect to be meaningful. In fact, the best ones rarely are.

- **Cultural Immersion**: connecting deeply with local customs, traditions, and communities. In Japan, instead of a modern hotel, we chose to stay in a traditional ryokan. We slipped into yukata robes, slept on tatami mats, and soaked in steaming onsen baths. Meals were served as multi-course kaiseki feasts, each dish presented like art. It was not just a place to stay; it was stepping into centuries of culture, and it left me with a richer understanding of Japan than any guidebook ever could.

- **Food and Culinary Exploration**: discovering a place through its flavors, markets, and kitchens. In Bali, we joined a cooking class that began with a trip to the local market. Surrounded by stalls piled high with spices, produce, and still-flapping fish, we learned how to choose the ingredients before heading back to the kitchen. By the time we sat down to eat, it was both a meal and a memory, and richer because we had helped create it.

- **Wildlife and Nature**: seeking out encounters with the natural world, whether on safari, birdwatching, or camping under the stars. Off the coast of South Australia, I slipped into the water with a colony of Australian sea lions. Instead of darting away, they swirled around me like underwater acrobats, blowing bubbles and tugging at my fins. It felt less like watching wildlife and more like being invited into their game.

- **Photography and Creativity**: chasing moments that inspire, from sweeping landscapes to small details. Over Shark Bay in Western Australia, we took a small plane to photograph the turquoise shallows and

> winding sandbars from above. Through the lens, the coastline transformed into patterns of color and texture that looked more like abstract art than geography.

This isn't a complete list, and your values will look different than mine. When I think about what I now seek in travel, three themes keep surfacing: the thrill of adventure, the wonder of wildlife, and the creativity of photography. Not every trip includes all three, but together they act as my compass, steering me toward the experiences that matter most.

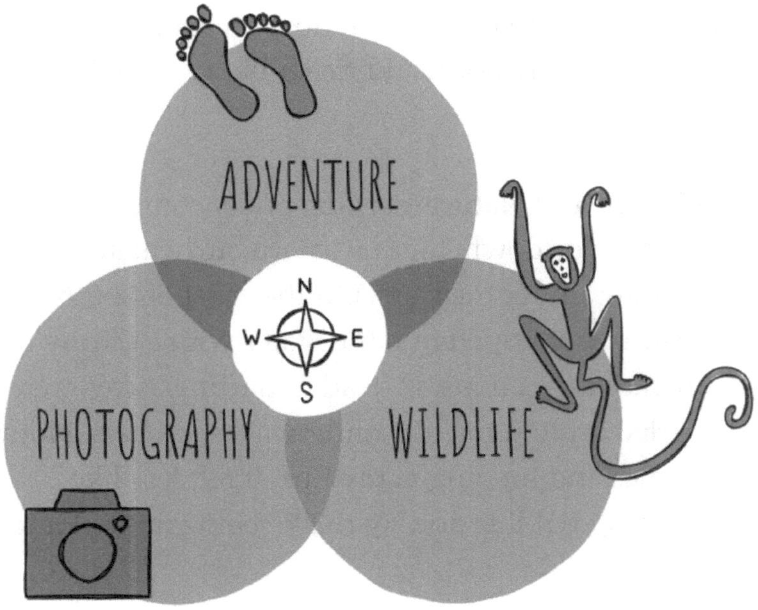

My North Star: adventurous travel with a focus on wildlife photography.

In Summary

Your travel values are the basis for all your choices about where to go and what to do. They are the compass that keeps you pointed toward trips that matter most and the filter that helps you say no to the ones that do not. When you align your Wanderlist with your values, your travels become more intentional, more fulfilling, and more memorable.

Now it is your turn. The next activity will help uncover your travel values, so your Wanderlist reflects not just the places you want to see, but the experiences that truly matter to you.

ACTIVITY

Discovering Your Travel Values

Your travel values are the compass for your Wanderlist. They will guide you toward the trips that matter most and away from the ones that do not. Take a few minutes to uncover what really drives you to travel.

Do not skip this activity. You must set your compass first for the rest of your Wanderlist to make sense.

---

1. **Set the scene**

   Find a quiet spot, grab a notebook, some sticky notes, or your favorite notetaking app, and give yourself 15–20 minutes. If you are doing this activity with a partner or family, start individually, then compare.

2. **Ask the big questions, such as**

   - What do I look forward to most when I travel?
   - Which trips have felt most satisfying, and why?
   - What makes me feel most alive when traveling?
   - What would I miss if travel was not part of my life?

3. **Spot your patterns**

   Look at your notes and highlight themes. Are some more important than others? Do any overlap?

   Think about your past travel experiences and how these values have influenced your choices and emotions. Consider moments when your values aligned perfectly with your travels and times when they may have been at odds.

4. **Choose your top values**

   Select two or three that matter most to you right now. These will become the foundation of your Wanderlist. Remember, values evolve. Revisit periodically to see if they have shifted.

Once you have completed this activity, you will have a shortlist of the travel values that define what "meaningful" looks like for you. Keep these handy, as they will shape every step of your Wanderlist Blueprint.

Recap of Step 1 - Discovering Your Values

Your values are the compass that keeps your travels on course. They point you toward the trips that matter most and help you avoid ones that do not.

In Step 1, you:

- Reflected on what really drives you to travel.
- Identified the values that guide your decisions.
- Built the foundation for your Wanderlist.

Keep these values handy; they will shape every step of your Wanderlist Blueprint.

Values are your compass.
They point you toward the trips that matter most.

Wanderlist Journey

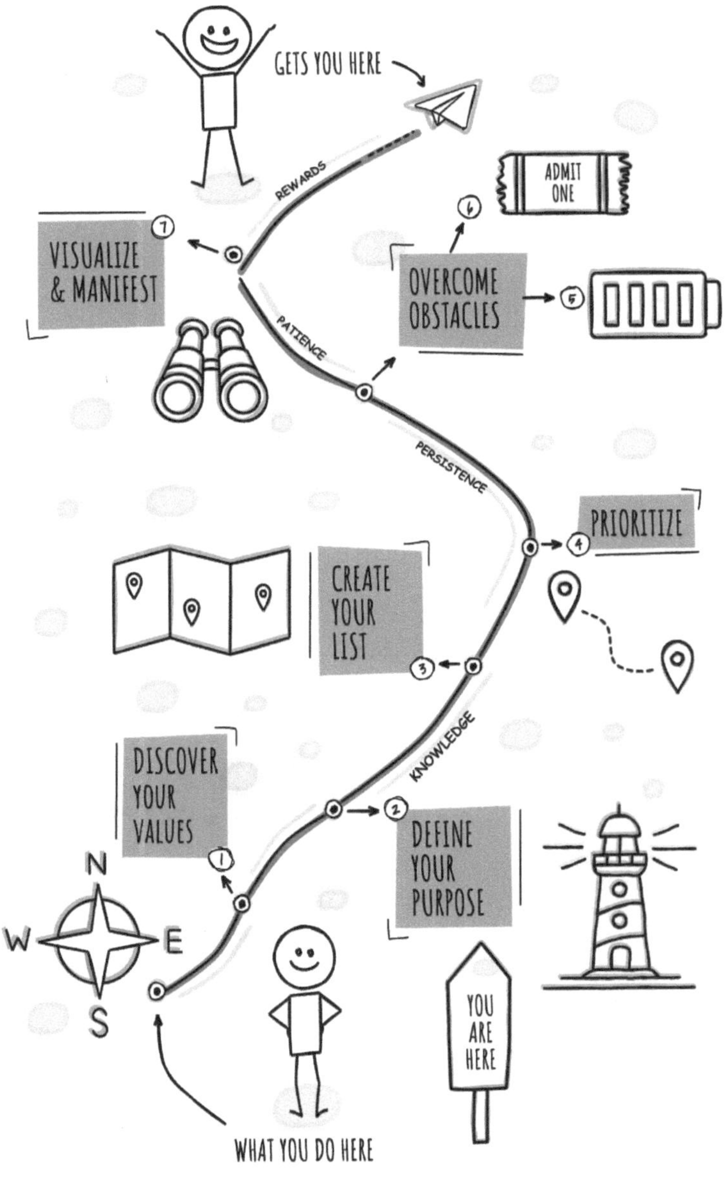

Step 2

DEFINING YOUR TRAVEL PURPOSE

If values are your compass, your purpose is your lighthouse, shining a light on where you truly want to go. This chapter focuses on helping you discover your "why"- the reason travel matters to you at all.

I first caught a glimpse of my purpose years ago at a work function. I was chatting with a group of colleagues when someone mentioned my travel website. Another person's eyes lit up. *"Wait, you're WhyWeWork? We booked a trip to Greece after seeing your photos!"*

This was before Instagram existed and before sharing images online was a common practice for everyone. I had always considered my site to be a personal project, a place dedicated to collecting stories and images. But that moment stopped me in my tracks. It was not just about me documenting my travels; it was about inspiring others to explore the world.

Capturing the World to Inspire Exploration

Over time, travel stopped being just about ticking off new places. It became about seeing the world through my camera and sharing that view with others. Photography lets me freeze fleeting moments and invite people into them, offering a glimpse of the awe I felt in that place.

People often ask if I sell or exhibit my photos. The truth is, the best reward is not likes or sales; it is when someone tells me they booked a trip because one of my photos made them want to see it for themselves.

That is my travel purpose: connecting people to places through images. Whether it is hiking the golden coastline of Abel Tasman in New Zealand or watching meerkats stand guard in the Makgadikgadi Pans in Botswana, I want others to feel the same awe I did and maybe be nudged to go find it themselves. That is what keeps me clicking the shutter.

Finding Your Purpose

Your purpose will not look like mine. Maybe it is adventure. Maybe it is learning. Maybe it is connection. Whatever it is, naming it will make your travel more meaningful.

In this next section, we will explore two powerful methods to help you define your purpose: the **Five Whys** technique, which uncovers the root of your motivations, and the **Is/Is Not** analysis, which is a clear framework that helps you articulate what travel means (and does not mean) to you. These tools will help you reflect on why you truly are keen to explore the world and how to align your travels with your personal values.

The Five Whys Method

One of the easiest ways to uncover your travel purpose is to keep asking yourself a simple question: *why?* And ask yourself not just once, but five times in a row. Each answer reveals a deeper layer, guiding you beyond surface-level motivations (*"I want to see new places"*) to the underlying desire (*"I want a life filled with stories, not routines"*).

Think of it like digging through layers of an onion. It is a little messy; sometimes it makes your eyes water, but it gets you closer to the core.

Here is what it might look like in practice:

1. **Why do I want to travel?**
   Because I want to relax and recharge.
2. **Why do I want to relax and recharge?**
   Because my day-to-day life feels overwhelming and stressful.
3. **Why do I want to escape stress?**
   Because it affects my health, and I do not feel like my best self.

4. **Why do I want to feel like my best self?**
   Because when I feel balanced, I am more patient and present.
5. **Why do I want that?**
   Because I want to return home from travel not just rested, but renewed, with energy I can carry back into everyday life.

By the end, your why becomes clearer. In this example, it is not just about getting away to relax; it is about using travel to reset, recharge, and come home renewed. That is a purpose you can build a Wanderlist around.

The Is/Is Not Method

Another way to reveal your travel purpose is to think about what it *is* and what it *is not*. Sometimes it is easier to get clarity by looking at both sides. Here is an example:

Travel Is	**Travel Is Not**
A chance to spend time with family and reconnect away from daily routines.	Being constantly plugged into work emails and social media.
A way to reset and recharge, even if it means sitting still in one beautiful place.	Rushing through a checklist of tourist sites just to say I've been there.

By the end, your why becomes clearer. Seeing both sides helps you cut through the clutter and focus on what travel really means to you. That is a purpose you can build a Wanderlist around.

In Summary

Defining your travel purpose is what gives meaning to every trip. It is the lighthouse that illuminates beyond the destinations on your list, guiding you towards the profound "why" underlying your Wanderlist. When you know your purpose, your travels become part of a bigger story that reflects who you are.

Now it is your turn. The next activity will help you find your travel purpose, so your Wanderlist is based on both where and why you want to go there.

ACTIVITY

Defining Your Purpose

Your travel purpose is the reason behind your Wanderlist. It gives meaning to your choices and helps you focus on what matters most.

Do not just skim this. Pause and do it now. Your Wanderlist will only make sense if you have uncovered the "why" behind it.

---

1. **Set the scene**

   Find a quiet moment where you will not be interrupted, maybe on a walk, over coffee, or with a journal. The key is to slow down and reflect on why travel really matters to you. If you are on the move, ensure that you have a way to record your thoughts. The important part is capturing your thoughts, not how you capture them. As with the first activity, if you are doing this with a partner or family, start individually, then compare.

2. **Ask yourself "why?" (five times)**

   Start with a simple question: *Why do I want to travel?* Note your first answer. Then ask yourself "why?" again. Keep going until you have asked it five times. Each answer will reveal a deeper level and bring you closer to the root cause.

3. **Create a list of what travel is and what it is not**

   On one side of a page, jot down what travel *is* for you. On the other side of the page, write what travel *is not* for you. There are no wrong answers if you are honest.

   For example:
   Travel *is* learning new things.
   Travel *is not* rushing from sight to sight just to tick boxes.

   The contrast will help you see what matters most.

4. **Spot the themes**

   Look back at both exercises. Are there recurring themes or ideas that repeat? These are clues to your deeper "why."

5. **Write your purpose statement**

   In two or three sentences, sum up your travel purpose. Keep it simple and personal, like "*My purpose is to travel in ways that connect me with nature and leave me feeling restored."*

Once you have completed this activity, you will have a clear sense of your travel purpose. Remember, this is not set in stone. Your purpose may shift as you do, so revisit it periodically and see what has changed.

Recap of Step 2 - Defining Your Purpose

Your values are the compass that keeps you pointed in the right direction. Your purpose is the lighthouse that shows you *why* you are heading there in the first place.

In Step 2, you:

- Explored two tools for uncovering your "why": the Five Whys and the Is/Is Not exercise.
- Named your travel purpose, the deeper reason behind your Wanderlist.

Keep this purpose close. It is what turns your Wanderlist from a checklist into a map that reflects who you are and why you explore.

Purpose is your lighthouse.
It lights the way toward what matters most.

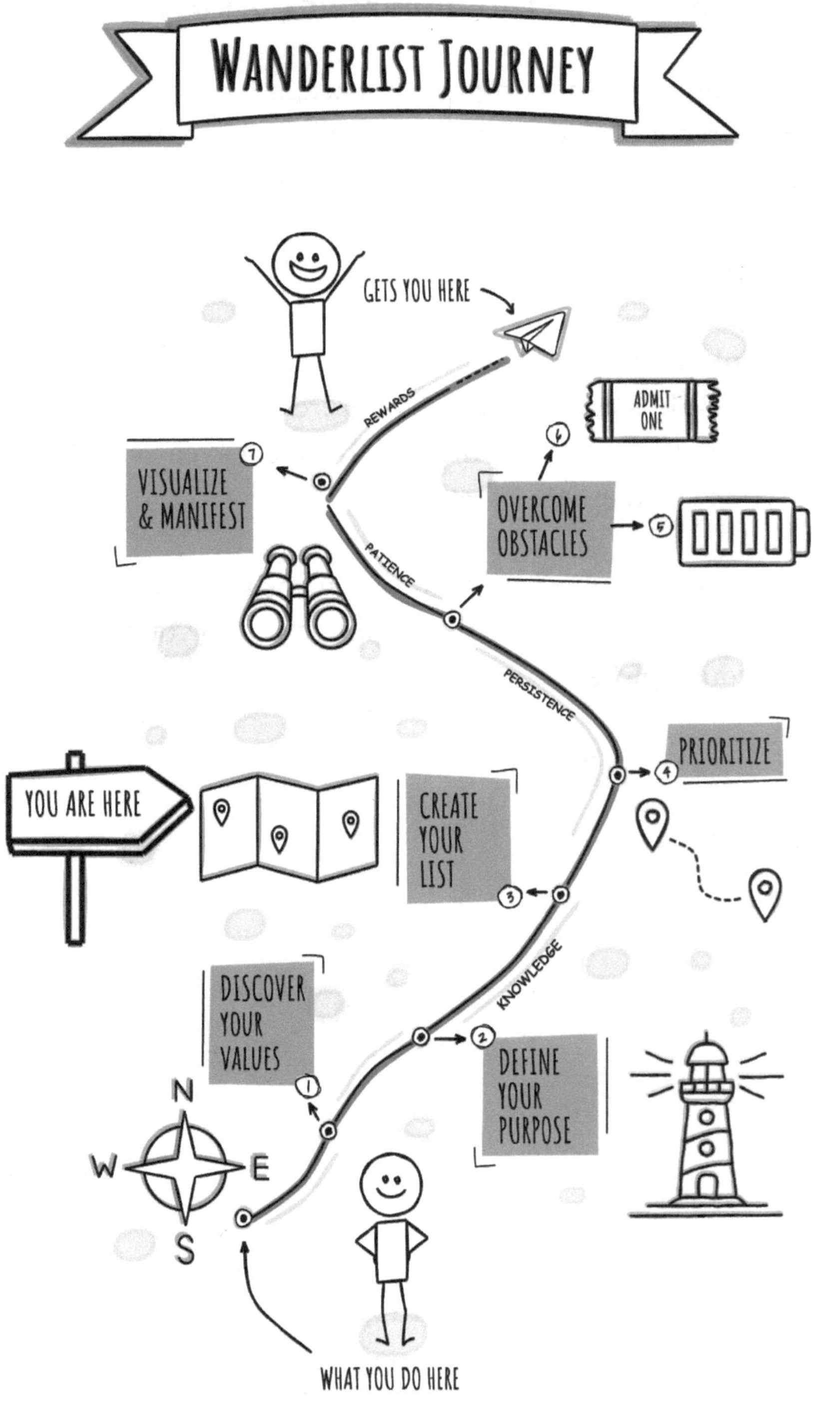
Wanderlist Journey
GETS YOU HERE
ADMIT ONE
REWARDS
VISUALIZE & MANIFEST
OVERCOME OBSTACLES
PATIENCE
PERSISTENCE
PRIORITIZE
YOU ARE HERE
CREATE YOUR LIST
KNOWLEDGE
DISCOVER YOUR VALUES
DEFINE YOUR PURPOSE
N
W
E
S
WHAT YOU DO HERE

Step 3

CREATING YOUR WANDERLIST

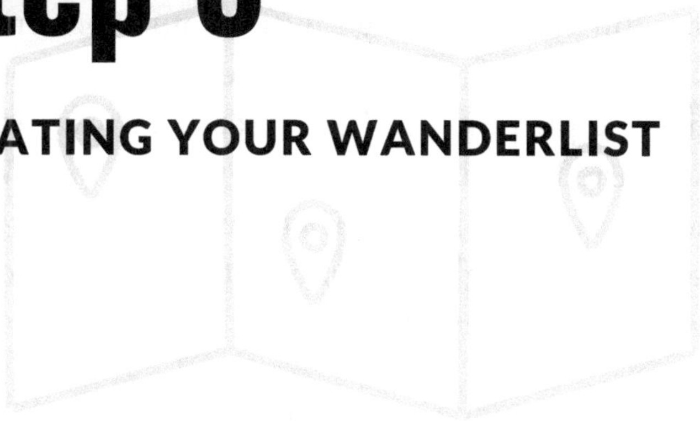

Our Wanderlist does not live on paper; it lives on a shared Google Map. Anytime we stumble across something intriguing, we drop in a pin. Just last night, after watching a YouTube video about a photography hide in Zambia, I added a new destination to the map. Over time, that map has become a patchwork of possibilities, dots scattered across continents, each one representing a spark of curiosity waiting its turn.

If values are your compass and purpose is your lighthouse, then your Wanderlist is where those sparks come together, a lightbulb moment that turns dreams into something you can map and navigate. This chapter is about creating that first version: not a perfect, final list, but a living, evolving brainstorm of ideas that excite you.

So, let us start building! Where will you drop your pins?

Identify Dream Destinations and Experiences

This is the fun part, dropping pins on your Wanderlist. But to keep it meaningful, your choices should tie back to the values and purpose you have already uncovered. Back when we started our list, the first pin was obvious. We dreamed of a safari in Africa. Then came the harder part. Do we add everything that sounds interesting or focus on places we think we can afford?

To help you sort through your list, here are a few things to consider when choosing your dream destinations and experiences.

Domestic Versus International Exploration

It is easy to believe that there are better destinations elsewhere. On flights from Australia to the U.S., I have sat next to Australians heading to Mexico for the beaches. Part of me wants to tell them they are flying the wrong way. Australia has some of the best beaches in the world, yet many Australians prefer to travel to overseas beaches.

It reminds me of a conversation I had with a bus driver in the Netherlands years ago. I was on my way to photograph the tulip fields. The driver struck up a conversation after hearing my accent and told me how his family rented a motorhome each summer to explore U.S. national parks. I had lived in the U.S. my whole life and had only been to one national park as a kid. I was embarrassed but also inspired. Our next trips were to Yosemite, Yellowstone, and Grand Teton.

This highlights the trap of viewing travel as a choice between domestic or international and assuming that extraordinary experiences can only be found abroad. The truth is, you can find extraordinary adventures almost anywhere once you know what you are looking for.

Popular Versus Off-the-Beaten-Path Destinations

Travel often tempts us to choose: do we head for the famous landmarks everyone knows, or do we seek the hidden corners few people have heard of? It is not about which is better; it is about what fits your values and purpose at that moment.

Take Uluru. This massive monolith in Australia's Red Centre is one of the country's icons, and for good reason. I spent a long weekend there that included a camel ride at sunrise and a luxury dining experience under a sky bursting with stars. Uluru is popular, accessible, and steeped in culture, and a reminder that sometimes the classics really are worth it.

Now contrast that with the Bungle Bungles in Western Australia. Getting there is part of the adventure: a six-hour drive from Kununurra, and a four-wheel drive is required for the river crossings. When we finally arrived, our "glamping" spot turned out to be a cluster of tents, a fire pit, and a big open-air dining room. That first evening we gathered around the fire, and we were the only independent travelers there. Every person we met asked the same two things. *"How did you arrive here on your own? And how did you even discover this place?"*

That is the difference. One place sits on postcards; the other makes people question how you got there at all. Both are unforgettable, and both have a place on a Wanderlist.

Sometimes you crave the icons, sometimes the hidden gems.

Expanding Beyond Your Comfort Zone

Some of the best memories come from the moments that scare you a little, the ones that force you past what feels comfortable. Two trips stand out for me.

The first was Tiger Beach in the Bahamas, a dive site famous for encounters with tiger sharks. The water was clear and calm, but nothing prepares you for the moment you drop in and are surrounded by dozens of sharks. At first, every instinct told me this was crazy. But then awe took over. Floating there, face-to-face with these powerful animals, was one of the most exhilarating hours of my life.

The second was hiking to see mountain gorillas in Uganda. After hours of slogging through mud and thick jungle at high altitude, slipping on vines, I finally gave in to my porter, who half-dragged me up the last mountain.

By the time we located the gorillas, I was utterly exhausted and covered in mud, but the experience was truly unforgettable. Sitting quietly as they moved through the forest, so close you could hear them breathe, was worth every grueling step.

Both experiences pushed me far beyond what felt easy. And that is the point: stepping outside your comfort zone often leads to the moments you will treasure most.

New Versus Tried and True

Most of the time, I chase new places. But a few destinations keep calling me back. Sabi Sands, next to South Africa's Kruger National Park, tops that list. I have been six times, even skipping other trips just for the chance to return.

On my last visit, I told our ranger I wanted to photograph cats. He nodded, then swerved the 4x4 off the road a few minutes later and, in his lovely South African accent, asked with a grin, *"Ah know you sed kets, but wot about wahld dawgs?"*

Wild dogs, or African painted dogs, are rare. There are only about 6,000 left in the wild, and I had only ever seen them once, for a fleeting moment. This time, we drove straight into a pack of twenty. They darted in every direction, a blur of energy and color. Even the rangers were giddy, which is how you know it is a special sighting.

Later that same day, we came across a pride of twenty-two lions sprawled across the savannah, cubs tumbling over each other in play. It was everything I had asked for, but it was the dogs I could not stop thinking about. That is why I keep going back. Sometimes the real magic is not in chasing the new but in returning to a place that still manages to surprise you.

Become an Expert in Research

Researching destinations is half the fun and half the challenge. I have lost count of how many nights I have fallen into a Google rabbit hole, tabs multiplying faster than I can read them. Right now, I have five open for Iceland alone: ferries, lodges, and points of interest. Add in the occasional YouTube binge of northern lights in Finnish Lapland or Antarctica vlogs, and suddenly hours have vanished.

That is the beauty of it. Research is not just logistics; it is discovery. Done well, it helps you uncover experiences you would never stumble across otherwise, and it makes sure the trips you dream about fit your values and purpose.

In this section, we will look at what to capture, how to stay organized, and fourteen different ways to dig up ideas for your Wanderlist.

What Information to Capture

When you are first building your Wanderlist, you do not need to know every detail. Just capture the basics. Think of it as two phases of research:

- **First Pass:** just enough to see if a place deserves a spot on your list.
- **Deep Dive:** the nitty-gritty details once you are serious about visiting a destination.

For your first pass, here are the things worth jotting down:

- **Destinations:** Start a simple list of places that spark your interest. For instance, you might consider Iceland for its puffins or Peru for Machu Picchu.
- **Season:** Note the best time to go. This might be tied to wildlife migrations (spirit bears in Canada in September), festivals (Cherry Blossom Festival in Japan in late March / early April), or simply good weather (Patagonia in November - March).
- **Cost:** Capture a rough idea. It does not need to be precise. Even a quick rating from $ (budget-friendly weekend in Vietnam) to $$$$$ (once-in-a-lifetime Antarctica voyage) will give you a sense.
- **Values and Purpose:** Ask yourself if this destination lines up with what matters to you. For example, if one of your values is wildlife, a safari in Kenya might rank higher than a trip to Paris.

That is it. Keep it light at this stage. The goal is to provide yourself enough information to compare options later (Step 4).

How to Organize Your Research

Once you have started gathering ideas, the trick is keeping them from vanishing into a mess of open tabs, screenshots, and random scraps of paper. The good news? There are plenty of ways to keep your Wanderlist ideas tidy, from slick digital tools to good old paper sticky notes. The best system is the one you will actually use.

Digital Tools

Most digital tools are built for collaboration, which makes them perfect if you are planning as a couple, family, or group of friends. Here are a few to try, depending on how you like to think:

- **Trello:** Great for visual thinkers. You can create a board with cards for each destination, add notes and checklists, and drag them around as you refine your list.
- **Evernote / Notion:** A good fit if you like notebooks. Store details, attach images, and tag ideas so they are easy to find later.
- **Mural / Miro / Freeform:** Best for creatives who want a blank canvas. Build interactive mood boards and brainstorm together in real time.

- **Pinterest:** Perfect for inspiration-driven planners. Pin photos, articles, and videos into boards for each destination.
- **Google Docs:** Best for note takers. Keep a shared list with links, descriptions, and comments.
- **Google Sheets:** Perfect for list makers. Build a simple table with columns for season, cost, and alignment with values.

Paper and Analog Methods

If you prefer hands-on planning, these old-school approaches can be just as powerful (and fun to do with others):

- **Travel Journal:** Write notes, paste photos, or sketch ideas.
- **Sticky Notes:** Jot one destination per note and move them around on a wall or board.
- **Vision Boards:** Collect images, quotes, and clippings into a collage.
- **Map with Pins:** Hang a wall map and drop in colored pins for each destination.

The point is not to master every tool. It is to pick the one that fits how you naturally think. If you are a visual person, Mural, Miro, or Freeform might inspire you. If you love lists, a spreadsheet will feel satisfying. If you are planning with others, lean into tools that make collaboration easy, so everyone's ideas have a place.

14 Ways to Research Destinations and Experiences

Before we dive into the 14 ways to research destinations and experiences, here is one quick tip to save yourself frustration later: However you like, save everything in one central place. Use the system you set up in the last section so your inspiration does not get lost in scattered bookmarks, folders, playlists, and screenshots.

1. **Watch Documentaries**

   This is one of my favorite research methods because documentaries are usually less biased than social media. The credits often list filming locations, guides, and even tour operators.

   That is precisely how Tonga landed on our Wanderlist. After watching *Tales by Light* and an episode of *60 Minutes* called *Humpback Heaven,* we spotted "Whale Swim Adventures" in the credits. Their trips book out fast, so we locked in a spot a year and a half in advance. What started as inspiration on the screen turned into one of our most unforgettable experiences: swimming with humpback whales in Tonga.

2. **Watch YouTube**

   YouTube is the second-most popular search engine after Google, and it is packed with travel vlogs and videos that give you a real sense of a destination.

When I was researching Norway, I searched for "orcas in Norway," "swimming with orcas," and "Norway vlog" and found hours of content that showed me what it is actually like to be there. The more I watched, the more the algorithm served up even better suggestions.

Pro Tip: Watch for logos on guides' clothing or vehicles. If the name or logo is unclear, take a screenshot and use Google Image Search to track it down.

3. **Use Social Media**

Scrolling social media is one of the fastest ways to spark travel ideas. TikTok, Instagram, and even Facebook groups can be goldmines when you follow the right pages, hashtags, or creators.

As a photographer, I have built lists of astrophotographers, wildlife shooters, and travel storytellers whose posts constantly feed me new inspiration. But here is the catch: social media is curated, and as we know, there's often a difference between Instagram and reality.

Take Lake Tekapo in New Zealand. On Instagram, the Milky Way perfectly arches over the Church of the Good Shepherd, with a lone photographer standing beneath the stars. In reality, the space was crowded with bus-loads of people using flashlights. Although the sky was breathtaking, the scene was far from serene. Social media can inspire your travels, but it pays to keep a sense of perspective. It is important to remember that the picture-perfect version is only half the story.

4. **Read Travel Blogs and Websites**

Travel blogs and websites can feel like sitting down with a friend who has already been where you want to go. They share the kind of small details and honest stories you will never find in a glossy brochure.

When we made a last-minute trip to Queensland's Atherton Tablelands, we decided to try and spot tree kangaroos. We spent two full days wandering without any luck, and by dinner on the second night, I was feeling discouraged. A quick internet search led me to a personal vlog that listed the best locations in the region for sightings. The next morning, we headed straight there and finally spotted the elusive marsupials.

5. **Listen to Podcasts**

Podcasts are a great way to get ideas and inspiration while doing other things like commuting, cooking, or even going for a walk. A quick search in your favorite podcast app for a destination or theme can surface gems you would never find in a guidebook.

When I had a long commute, I used the time to listen to *The Nature Photo Guys*. It felt like having a conversation with fellow photographers, swapping tips and ideas for destinations.

Pro Tip: download a few episodes before a flight or road trip. It is an easy way to turn downtime into travel research time.

6. **Participate (or Lurk) in Travel Forums**

Travel forums and groups are like digital campfires, places where travelers swap stories, vent about mishaps, and share the kind of tips you will not find in a guidebook. Whether it is Reddit's r/travel, niche Facebook groups, or smaller communities, they can be goldmines for inspiration and practical advice.

Before our first trip to Kenya, I spent hours lurking in the old Lonely Planet Thorn Tree Forum (sadly shut down in 2021). That community taught me things guidebooks skipped, like how long visas really took and what counted as a fair tip.

Forums can also help during your trip. In Friday Harbor, I joined a local Facebook group for whale sightings. One evening, someone posted that orcas were cruising the coastline. We dropped everything, rushed out, and caught them gliding past at sunset. Without that group, we would have missed one of the most magical moments of the trip.

7. **Read Travel Magazines and Guidebooks**

   There is something timeless about flipping through glossy pages or dog-earing a guidebook. Magazines spark ideas with features on new and trending destinations, while guidebooks dig into the nuts and bolts: history, culture, attractions, and how to get around.

   Two decades ago in France, we leaned heavily on Rick Steves' guidebooks. We trusted his hotel picks, followed his self-guided walking tours, and even skipped a three-block queue at the Orsay Museum thanks to one of his tips. You will have to read the book yourself to learn that one.

8. **Speak with Other Travelers**

   Some of the best travel tips do not come from guidebooks or Google. They come from the people you bump into along the way.

   On a photography tour in Churchill, Canada, we met a woman from Italy with an adventurous spirit. In the middle of a polar bear search, she handed us a business card with a snow monkey photo on it. She had been to Japan the year before and happily shared her tips for Jigokudani. That one conversation not only inspired us to add snow monkeys to our Wanderlist, but it also gave us the idea to make our own photo cards, which now include a QR code linking back to our website.

9. Ask the Locals for Recommendations

Locals almost always know the best spots, the tucked-away cafés, the stunning viewpoints, and the hidden gems that never make it into a guidebook. The trick is to ask in a way that gives them something to work with. Mention your travel dates, your interests, or even a meal you loved last time.

On a flight to Kona, I struck up a conversation with my seatmate, who lived in Hilo. I told him how much I had enjoyed the pancakes at Ken's House of Pancakes on my last trip. He grinned and said, *"You have to try the Hawaiian Sweet Bread French Toast at Hawaiian Style Café in Waimea."* It was well off the tourist path, and we were the only non-locals in the place. The French toast was so good we went back twice.

10. Attend Travel Trade Shows

Travel trade shows are like candy stores for wanderlisters. Booth after booth is filled with destinations, tour operators, and tourism reps eager to show you why their corner of the world deserves a spot on your list.

I was determined to make the most of my weekends while working in Malaysia. A travel trade show in

Kuala Lumpur provided me with much-needed inspiration. I wandered the aisles, snapped photos of intriguing displays (instead of hauling home brochures I would just toss), and scribbled down notes about discounts. A few weeks later, one of those notes turned into a flight to Langkawi for a long weekend in search of dusky monkeys.

Trade shows are a fantastic way to gather fresh ideas, obtain insider tips, and sometimes even score deals, even if you do not book anything immediately.

11. Read Reviews

Reviews can be gold, but they can also mislead. Understanding the nuances is crucial, though.

On a work trip to Bangalore, I tacked on a stop in the Maldives. It was low season for weather but peak season for manta rays, so I hunted for somewhere close to Hanifaru Bay. I found a place with a 50% discount, a glowing 4.5-star TripAdvisor rating, and reviews that sounded delightful. *"Perfect,"* I thought.

The reality was a mix of half-completed construction, a total lack of customer service, and a cold, dreary buffet on repeat. After the trip, I dug deeper and finally found the truth buried in one-star reviews: guests were offered $50 credits for posting something positive. That experience taught me to look past the headline rating. Scan for patterns across reviews, pay attention to what people consistently mention, and think about whether their travel style matches yours. The details matter more than the stars.

Pro Tip: Filter reviews by the season you will be traveling in or by traveler type (solo, couple, or family). It gives you a more accurate picture of what your stay might look like.

12. Contact a Travel Agent

With so much information online, it is tempting to plan everything yourself. Usually, that can work fine. But for tricky destinations, a specialist travel agent can be the difference between a smooth trip and a nightmare.

When we planned a trip to Madagascar in 2011, I started with the Bradt Guide. Buried in its pages was a mention of Rainbow Tours in the UK, the same people who had literally written the book. Who better to call?

At first, I questioned their recommendations. Were multiple buffer days in Antananarivo and a dedicated guide *really* necessary? Is that just wasting precious vacation time and adding to the expense?

Then the flight schedules began to change, with some flights departing a few hours early and others experiencing a two-day delay there. Suddenly, those buffer days and our local guide became priceless. Rainbow Tours had already built flexibility into our plan, so instead of panicking, we just kept traveling.

That trip taught me that, although it is convenient to rely on Google and DIY planning, there are instances when an expert's advice is invaluable. For destinations where logistics are tough, travel agents do not just book your trip; they help make sure the trip happens.

13. Take a Research Trip

Think of it as a tasting menu for travel. A research trip lets you sample a little bit of everything before deciding what deserves a full serving later. They are especially handy when you want to cover a lot of ground quickly and figure out which places are worth a longer stay.

We once jumped on an incredible bargain: a 7-night Western Caribbean cruise for just $250 per person. The ship was not fancy, but the itinerary took us to five islands we had never visited. Each stop was only a day, yet it was enough to know which islands we wanted to return to and which ones we could cross off the list.

14. Use Generative AI

AI tools like ChatGPT, Microsoft Copilot, and Google Gemini are changing the way we plan travel. They can brainstorm destinations, suggest itineraries, compare hotels, or even help you find the best photography spots. The key is knowing how to use them and when to double-check.

I learned these lessons firsthand during that extended work trip to Malaysia in 2023. At home, I usually cook, but being on the road meant finding a new place to eat every night. Almost jokingly, I asked ChatGPT to strategize my weekly dinner plans. I gave it my preferences, budget, and the requirement that everything be within walking distance.

It worked beautifully on paper. In reality, a couple of the restaurants had closed, and one "walking distance" suggestion involved a twenty-minute detour across a highway. It was a good reminder that while AI can be helpful, it is not foolproof. Always cross-check with up-to-date sources like Google Maps, reviews, or local advice.

Generative AI has the potential to transform travel research and planning. Ask it to brainstorm destinations that match your values, suggest activities for a free day in a city, or draft a first-pass itinerary. The trick is to treat it like a creative partner, not an oracle.

In Summary

Your Wanderlist is more than a list. It is a place to gather all those eureka moments as you have them.
At this stage, your Wanderlist does not need to be neat or final. It is about brainstorming freely, dropping pins, and noticing the patterns that connect back to what matters most. Over time, those scattered sparks will take shape,

and your Wanderlist will evolve into a guide you can follow.

Now it is your turn. The next activity will help you capture your sparks of curiosity and start shaping them into a Wanderlist that is wide open, inspiring, and brimming with possibility.

ACTIVITY

Creating Your Wanderlist

This is your chance to brainstorm freely. There are no wrong answers here, just ideas, sparks, and "what ifs" that deserve a place outside your head.

Do not put this off. Your Wanderlist only comes to life once you get those first ideas down. If you are planning with a partner, family, or group, create your lists individually first and compare notes later so everyone's voice gets heard. You may be surprised at what overlaps and what does not.

---

1. **Set the scene**

   Treat this like a game. Find a fun location, play some music, and grab a few snacks. Pick a way to record your ideas that feels natural; you could use sticky notes on the wall, a travel journal, a shared Google Map, or a spreadsheet. Use the simplest tool that makes it easy (and enjoyable) for you, and anyone you are planning with, to dream big and build together.

2. **Build your list**

   Start adding destinations and experiences. Do not filter yet; just create your list. A little detail helps, especially for the next steps:

   - **Name**: Cities, countries, landmarks, festivals, or experiences. (Example: Kyoto cherry blossoms, Serengeti migration.)
   - **Time of Year**: When you imagine going. (Example: Patagonia in November for hiking, or Iceland in June for puffins.)
   - **Cost**: Rough estimate, using $, $$, and $$$ to keep it simple.

3. **Add a wildcard**

   Think of one destination or experience you did not write down because it felt too far-fetched, too expensive, too long, or too challenging. Write it anyway. These are often the trips that matter most.

Once you have completed this activity, you will have an initial list of your travel dreams, concrete enough to build on, flexible enough to evolve. Your Wanderlist is not meant to be static. It is a living, breathing map of your dreams that will grow and shift as you find new sparks of inspiration. The important part is to start. Once the first pins are down, the rest will follow.

Recap of Step 3 - Creating Your Wanderlist

Your Wanderlist is the map that turns your values and purpose into something you can navigate. It will never be complete. It is a living, breathing collection of ideas that will keep evolving as you do.

In Step 3, you:

- Learned how to align dream destinations and experiences with your values and purpose.
- Explored various ways to spark inspiration and research, from documentaries and blogs to podcasts, forums, and even generative AI.
- Discovered simple ways to organize your research so it is easy to refine and return to.

Keep this list alive. Your Wanderlist is a record of the most important adventures in your future. Add to it, revisit it, and let it grow.

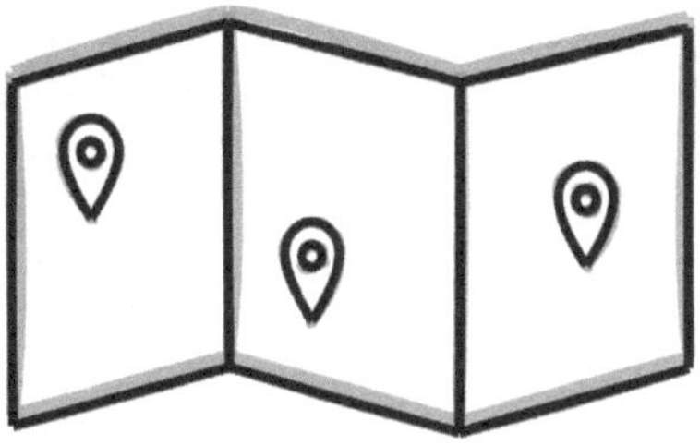

Your Wanderlist is your map, where sparks of curiosity gather and adventures begin to take shape.

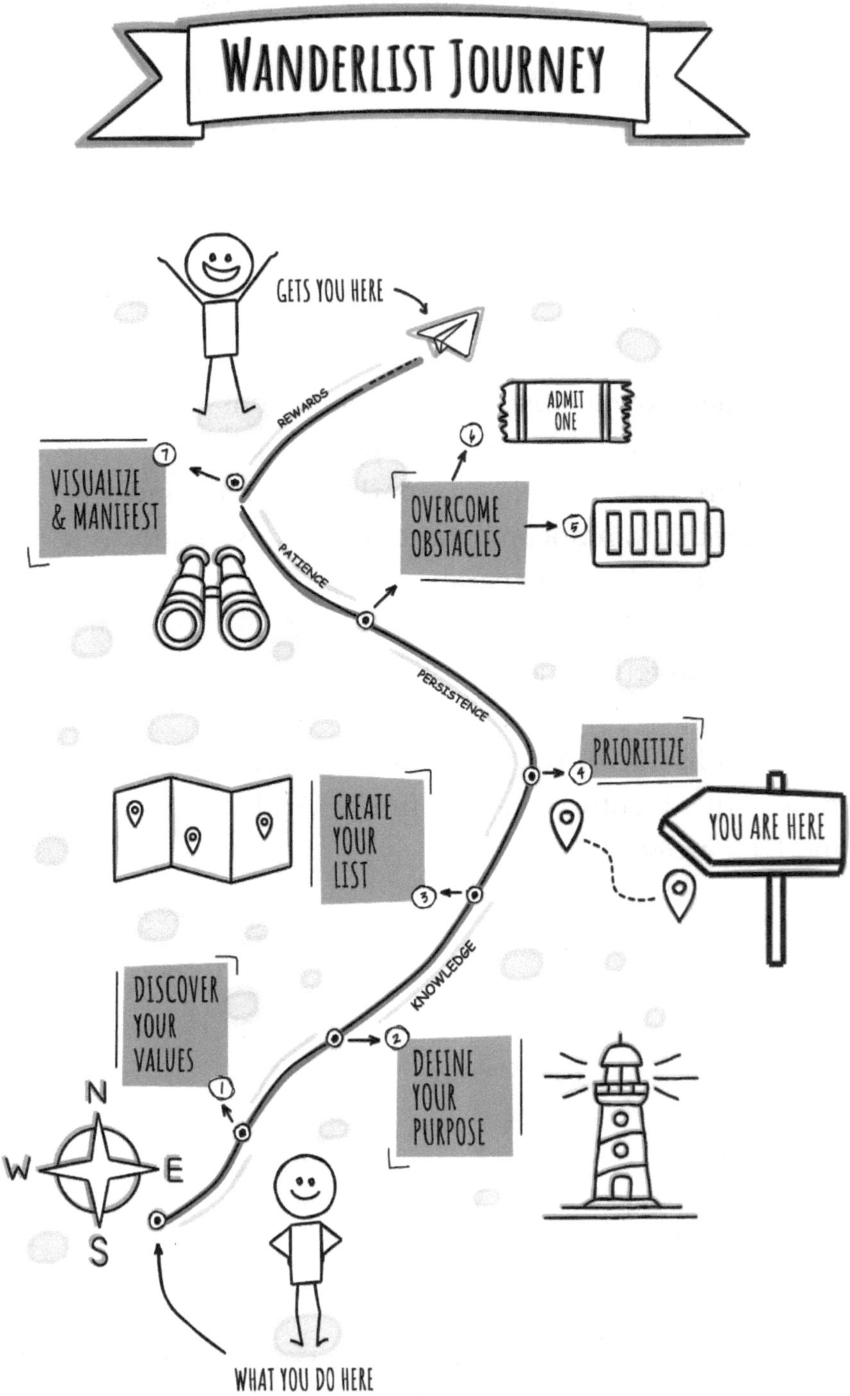
WANDERLIST JOURNEY
GETS YOU HERE
REWARDS
ADMIT ONE
6
7
VISUALIZE & MANIFEST
OVERCOME OBSTACLES
5
PATIENCE
PERSISTENCE
PRIORITIZE
4
YOU ARE HERE
CREATE YOUR LIST
3
KNOWLEDGE
DISCOVER YOUR VALUES
1
2
DEFINE YOUR PURPOSE
N
W
E
S
WHAT YOU DO HERE

Step 4

PRIORITIZING YOUR WANDERLIST

When the world stopped and Australia sealed itself off during COVID, we could not travel for two years. The absence of international and spontaneous getaways left us with only daydreams and a growing stash of unused annual leave and travel budget. But when the world finally opened again, we did not waste time wondering where to go. We already knew. Sitting right there on our Wanderlist was the pin that had been there for years: Antarctica. It had always felt out of reach, too big a splurge, and too difficult to fit into annual leave. But because we had our list and knew our priorities, we were ready the moment the chance arrived.

If your values serve as your compass, your purpose acts as the lighthouse, and your Wanderlist functions as the map, then prioritization becomes your route. It helps you sort through the noise, balance short-term and long-term goals, and make sure the trips you take are the ones that matter most right now. This chapter is about turning an overwhelming list into a clear path forward.

Prioritize Your Ideas

Now comes the challenging part: putting your Wanderlist in order. A map full of pins is exciting, but without some way to prioritize, it can feel overwhelming. Over the years, I have borrowed a few simple decision-making tools (the same ones I once used in consulting) and adapted them for travel. Think of them as shortcuts to help you sort through competing ideas and figure out what to say yes to first. Some trips are quick wins; others are dreams that take years of planning. The following tools help you spot the difference.

The Must/Could/Should/Won't Method

The MoSCoW method (funny name, simple idea) just means putting each destination or experience into one of four buckets: **M**ust, **S**hould, **C**ould, and **W**on't.

At this stage, do not worry about time, money, or logistics. This is not about what you can afford next year or how much annual leave you have got in the bank. It is about meaning. Which trips feel most deeply connected to your values and purpose? Which ones are nice-to-haves, and which do not fit at all? We will bring budget and timing into the picture later.

- **Must-do** → The non-negotiables. These are the trips that define your why. They align tightly with your values and purpose, and you would be heartbroken to miss them.
- **Should-do** → Important, meaningful, but not quite deal-breakers if they do not happen. They will enrich your Wanderlist and help bring your vision to life, but you could swap them out if something else rises higher.
- **Could-do** → Nice-to-haves. Fun additions that might surprise you, but you will not feel incomplete if they wait a while.
- **Won't-do** → Just as important as saying yes is deciding what does not belong. These are the trips that do not fit your style, values, or purpose right now.

This method provides an initial assessment of clarity, enabling you to identify the ideas that stand out the most when stripped of everything except your values and purpose. And sometimes "should" does not just mean meaningful. For example, it could also mean time-sensitive. For me, swimming with orcas in Norway or Mexico is a "should" right now, because I know it is the kind of experience that will be harder to enjoy if I wait until I am older or less fit. This urgency serves as a reminder that certain dreams deserve a front-row seat, not a spot on the someday shelf.

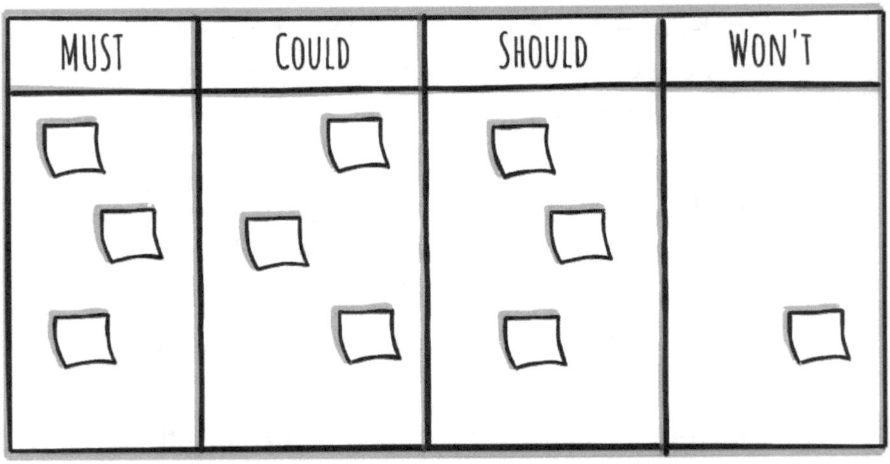

The 2x2 Grid Method

Some trips are quick wins. Others are the kind you daydream about for years. A simple 2x2 grid helps you sort the difference by weighing two things: **cost** and **complexity**.

- **Cost** runs from left to right, from budget-friendly on the left to splurge-worthy on the right.
- **Complexity** runs from easy, low-planning trips at the bottom to the logistically tricky ones at the top.

Where a trip lands depends on your circumstances. For example, camping would sit high on the complexity axis for me (I do not own gear and lack the know-how), but it might be low for someone who camps every summer.

Once you start plotting trips, you will see four quadrants emerge.

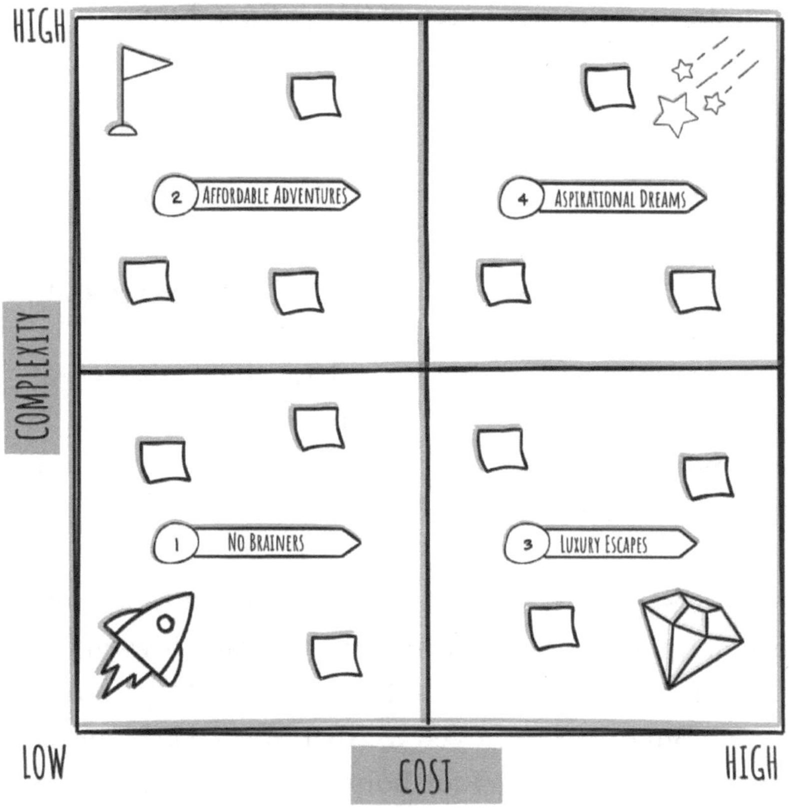

- **Quadrant 1: No Brainers (Low Cost, Low Complexity)**
  These are the straightforward, cheap, simple trips you can pull off quickly. For me, nearby national parks fall into this category. They are affordable, accessible, and always rewarding.
- **Quadrant 2: Affordable Adventures (Low Cost, High Complexity)**
  These take more planning, but they do not break the bank. Hiking New Zealand's Abel Tasman Coast Track

belongs here. It is budget-friendly but requires sorting tide schedules, transport, and accommodation long in advance.

- **Quadrant 3: Luxury Escapes (High Cost, Low Complexity)**
  Trips that are simple to book but come with a hefty price tag. A Baltic Sea cruise landed here for me; I could have it booked in an hour, but the cost put it in splurge territory.
- **Quadrant 4: Aspirational Dreams (High Cost, High Complexity)**
  These are the white whales, the trips that truly excite you. For me, this was visiting an emperor penguin colony in Antarctica, which is costly and complicated but would be unforgettable.

What is eye-opening is how trips can shift quadrants over time. Fiji, for example, sat firmly in Quadrant 4 when I lived in the U.S. because of the long flights, jet lag, and high cost. But once we moved to Australia, it suddenly slid to Quadrant 3: just a four-hour flight away and much more doable.

Sometimes you can even nudge a trip into a different box with a little creativity. Take Brooks Lodge in Alaska. Normally it is a classic Quadrant 4: you must enter a lottery 1.5 years in advance (with 8,000 other keen travelers), and the lodge rates are not cheap. But if you are willing to camp and take a ferry instead of the seaplane, you can avoid the lottery and shave off a giant chunk of the cost, moving it closer to Quadrant 1 or 2.

That is the beauty of the grid: it helps you see which adventures are easy wins, which ones require saving or planning, and which are dreams for another day. And when your values and purpose steer the plotting, the picture that emerges is uniquely yours.

The Travel Scorecard

Sometimes it is difficult to choose between two (or ten) amazing ideas. This is where a simple scorecard comes in handy. Think of it as a tool to provide structure around your gut feelings.

- **Feasibility**: How realistic is this trip to pull off? (Think distance, logistics, visas, fitness, and gear.)
- **Desirability**: How badly do you want to go? (This is your heart vote.)
- **Viability**: How well does it fit your budget and schedule?

	FEASIBILITY	DESIRABILITY	VIABILITY	TOTAL
LOCATION 1				
LOCATION 2				
LOCATION 3				
LOCATION 4				
LOCATION 5				

Give each idea a quick score. You do not need to overthink it. A simple 1–5 works just fine. If you are a details person, stretch it to 1–10. The point is not precision; it is perspective.

Here is an example of what it could look like to compare two destinations for a September/October trip:

	Feasibility	Desirability	Viability	Total
Bali	6-hour flight, cheap fares, lots of hotels, visa on arrival **8/10**	Beaches, culture, food, spa, dry season, crowded due to school holidays **6/10**	Ideal for 5-7 days, flight times are good for work **8/10**	**22/30**
Hawaii	10-hour flight + connection, more expensive, ESTA required for entry **7/10**	Warm but humid, some rain, volcanoes, beaches, surfing **6/10**	Higher costs, poor exchange rate, need 7-10 days **3/10**	**16/30**

According to the numbers, Bali edges out Hawaii, mainly because of lower cost and more predictable weather. That doesn't mean Hawaii is off the table, it just means Bali is a better fit for this scenario. Save Hawaii for another season and use frequent flyer points to reduce the cost.

The takeaway: the scorecard does not crown a winner; it just helps you spot the trade-offs. Think of it like a tiebreaker in your own head, a way to see which trips are easier to say "yes" to now and which ones might need a bit more saving, planning, or courage.

The Bull's-Eye Diagram Method

Think of your Wanderlist like a dartboard. The bull's-eye is for the trips that matter most, the ones that are closest to your values and purpose. The middle rings are for ideas that are still important but not quite as urgent, and the outer ring is for "someday" dreams.

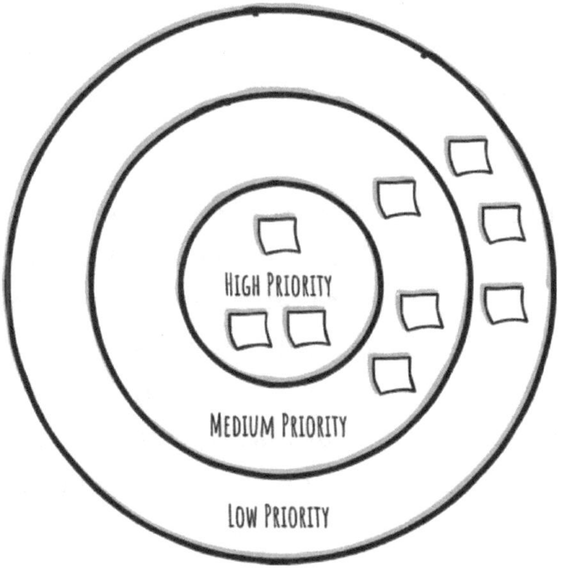

Start with your list and place each destination or experience in one of the circles:

- **Bull's-eye (high priority):** The trips you are most excited about right now, the ones that feel deeply aligned with your compass and lighthouse.
- **Middle ring (medium priority):** Ideas you want to do, but they can wait until the timing, budget, or circumstances line up better.

- **Outer ring (low priority):** Dreams for "later." They are still meaningful, but they do not need your immediate focus.

The beauty of this method is its simplicity. Just seeing your ideas on the target can help clarify what is calling to you now versus what can wait. And remember, nothing in the outer ring is off the table. It is just not at the center of your attention today.

In Summary

There is no single "right" way to prioritize your Wanderlist. The trick is finding the method (or mix of methods) that works best for you. You might start with MoSCoW to sort ideas into musts, shoulds, and coulds. From there, a 2x2 grid or a scorecard can help you weigh cost, complexity, or timing. Or maybe you will prefer the bull's-eye diagram to see what feels most urgent right now.

Each tool is just a different lens for looking at the same list. Use them together or on their own, whatever helps you see more clearly what matters most. Once you have done that, your Wanderlist stops being a pile of "somedays" and starts becoming a roadmap for trips that truly fit your values, purpose, and dreams.

Now it is your turn. The next activity will help you sift through the noise and put your Wanderlist in order. Some trips will rise to the top, others will wait their turn, and that is okay. It does not need to be perfect, just enough to show you where to start.

ACTIVITY

Prioritizing Your Wanderlist

You have got your values, your purpose, and your list. Now it is time to put some order to it.

Do not just skim this; do it now. Your Wanderlist only becomes useful when you know which trips to focus on first.

---

1. **Sort your list**

   Grab your ideas and drop them into four piles: must-do, should-do, could-do, and won't-do. Do not overthink logistics or money just yet. This is about meaning. Which trips tug at you the hardest? Which ones feel nice but are not essential? And which ones just do not fit right now?

2. **Map the "musts" and "shoulds"**

   Take the must-do and should-do piles and plot them on a simple 2x2 grid. Use cost on the horizontal axis (budget-friendly to splurge) and complexity on the vertical (easy to tricky). Sticky notes work great here.

3. **Step back and review**

   Look at what is on your grid. Notice patterns. Some trips may shift quadrants depending on your situation. You can sometimes nudge a trip into a new box by adjusting how you do it (camping instead of a lodge, traveling in shoulder season, etc.).

4. **Decide where to start**

   Here is the fun part: pick your first move. You could use the bull's-eye method and circle what feels most urgent. Or you could do what Andy and I do. The last time we could not decide between four destinations, I devised a dinner game: *"On three, we both blurt out our top two."* We laughed when the same two came up, just in a different order.

Once you have completed this activity, you will have a clear idea of what you want and where to start. Your priorities will change, and that is okay. What you have done here is give yourself a starting route. You now know which adventures to pursue first and which ones can wait for their turn. The rest will fall into place as you go.

Recap of Step 4 - Prioritizing Your Wanderlist

Prioritization is your route. It is what turns a pile of "somedays" into a clear path forward.

In Step 4, you:

- Explored simple tools for sorting your list, from MoSCoW categories to grids, scorecards, and the Bull's-Eye.
- Balanced short-term adventures with long-term dreams, making space for both what is urgent now and what can wait.

With your priorities in focus, your Wanderlist is no longer just a brainstorm. It is a roadmap aligned with your values and purpose, ready to guide your next move.

Priorities are your route. It is the way from "someday" to "next."

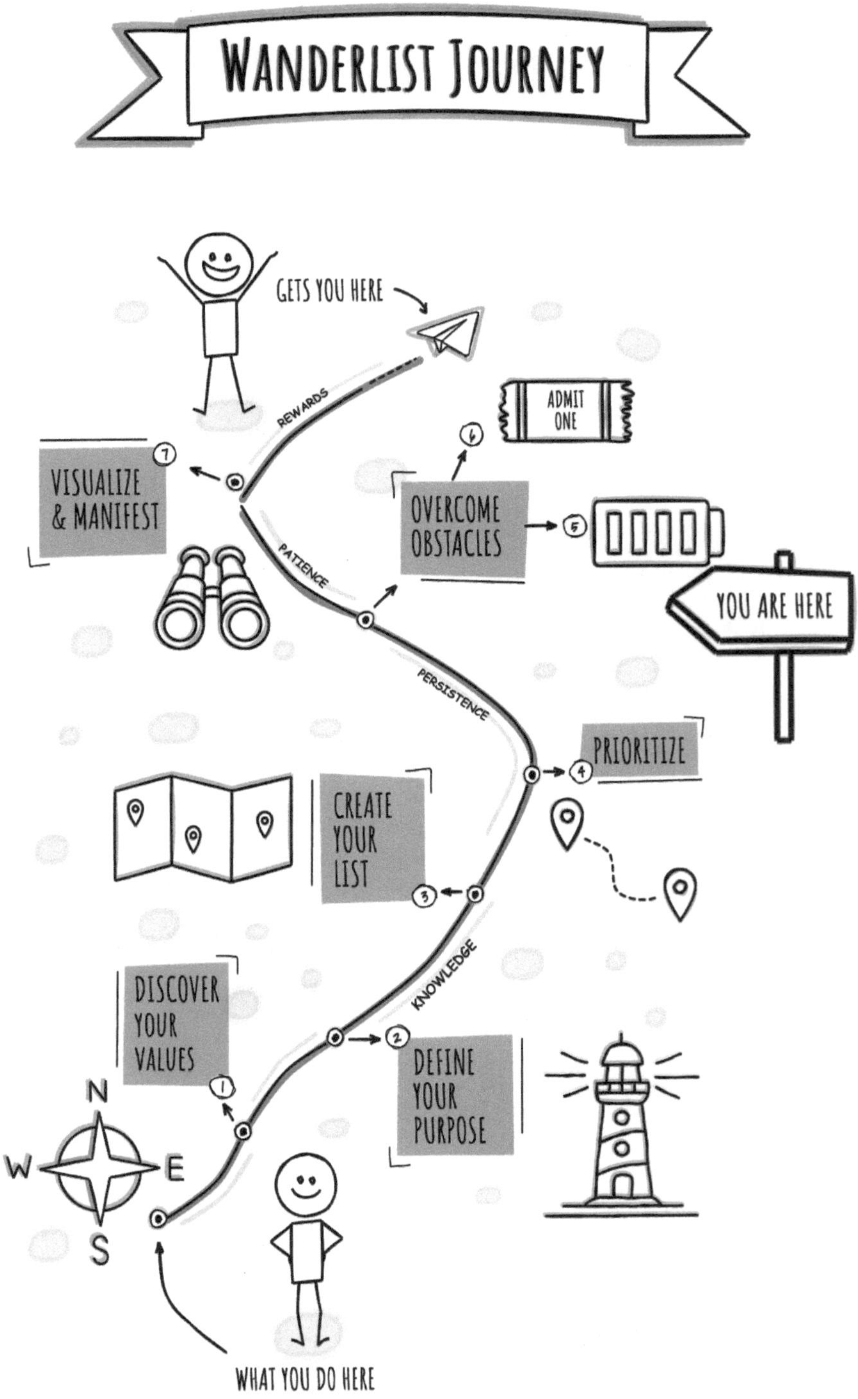
WANDERLIST JOURNEY
GETS YOU HERE
REWARDS
ADMIT ONE
7
VISUALIZE & MANIFEST
6
OVERCOME OBSTACLES
5
PATIENCE
YOU ARE HERE
PERSISTENCE
4
PRIORITIZE
CREATE YOUR LIST
3
KNOWLEDGE
DISCOVER YOUR VALUES
1
2
DEFINE YOUR PURPOSE
N
W
E
S
WHAT YOU DO HERE

Step 5

OVERCOMING FINANCIAL OBSTACLES

A few years ago, I was back at work after a long weekend camping at Wilson's Prom in Victoria. Over lunch, a colleague told me she wished she could travel more, just like me. We had the same job, probably similar salaries, but very different habits. I usually brought leftovers from home. She bought sushi and at least two lattes a day and collected designer shoes and handbags. A little math on a napkin told the story. Her "small treats" added up to more than $7,000 a year (not including the shoes and handbags!), a sum substantial enough to finance a few remarkable journeys.

This chapter is about building the resources that make your Wanderlist possible. We will cover two sides of the equation: how to save money for travel and how to spend less while you are out there. No guilt trips, no "skip every coffee forever" or "stay in hostels to save on accommodations." We will focus on practical systems and small adjustments that can free up more money for the things that truly really matter, such as adventures you will remember long after the latte foam fades.

How to Save Money for Travel

Dream trips do not just appear out of thin air; they are funded one decision at a time. The real magic is the compound effect: small changes continuously repeated that quietly stack up over time. The small choices you make every day can add up to a plane ticket or even an entire holiday.

This is not about extreme frugality or giving up everything you enjoy. It is about building smart habits and finding systems that put money aside for what matters most. Over the years, we have tested plenty of approaches, and some have become tried-and-true tactics that consistently fill our travel fund.

Here are 13 tactics I have embraced to turn my travel dreams into attainable realities.

As you read through these tactics, keep an eye on the **Wanderlist Watts (⚡)** shown after each tactic. Each one illustrates how small savings can add up over time. Do not worry about the exact amounts or the currency; it is the idea that matters. Small shifts here and there can make a huge difference in how much you can afford to travel.

1. Scrutinize Your Spending and Make a Budget

Before you can start saving, you need to know where your money is going. Track your expenses for a month or two, and you will start to see patterns and opportunities to cut back.

Once you have that picture, set yourself a budget. Some apps suggest spending a percentage of your income, but here is the trap: when your income goes up, so does your spending. I prefer a fixed dollar cap. For example, I aim to keep food costs under $1,000 (USD) a month. That way, any extra income flows straight into the travel fund.

The trick is to keep checking in. Over time, I noticed our food expenses creeping up. The culprits? Meal kits and grocery delivery had been quietly increasing in cost. The monthly audit made it obvious, and with a few tweaks I got things back on track:

- Swapped to dinner-only meal kits, which cut costs but kept the quality and convenience.
- Switched to a "two-stop" grocery run, getting basics at a discount chain, and then anything I could not find at the regular store.
- Discontinued grocery delivery entirely.

That one category alone freed up hundreds a month. The lesson? An audit is not a one-time task. It is a monthly check-in that helps you spot creeping costs and keep your savings pointed where you want them: toward travel.

Eliminate $200 per month of "budget creep" → $2,400 per year

2. Cancel Subscriptions

Subscriptions are sneaky. Streaming platforms, apps, gyms, software - it is almost as if they rely on you forgetting you signed up. Over time, those small charges can add up to serious money that could be going toward your travels. Go through your statements and ask: *Do I use this? Would I miss it?* If the answer is no, cancel it.

We once signed up for a free Audible trial and then promptly forgot about it. Six months later, we realized we had been paying for something neither of us was using. Since then, I have adopted a new rule: cancel trials as soon as I sign up. You can always reactivate later. And if it is a discounted offer you want to keep, set a calendar reminder before the renewal date. Little cuts like this are painless, but they free up real money.

Trim $50 per month in unused apps and services → $600 per year

3. Eat at Home

Dining out and ordering in are fun and convenient, but these small, frequent charges add up quickly.

Back in 2004, Andy and I were living in Chicago and dreaming about Africa. When we sat down to look at our spending, one thing jumped off the page: how much we were spending on dining out and delivery services. So, we made a deal. For six months, we would eat almost every meal at home. We even deleted our food delivery accounts to avoid temptation.

The result? The money we saved covered our entire annual travel budget, including that first big Africa trip.

Cooking at home might feel like a lot of work and may not feel as exciting as going out. If time is your concern, try meal prep. If decision fatigue is your issue, use an AI meal planner. If vibe is your struggle, plan theme nights and invite friends over; just have them bring something to keep the budget in check. When you connect meals to something bigger, like funding your dream safari or a flight to Paris, it becomes a habit worth savoring.

⚡ *Skip $30 takeaway twice per week → $3,120 per year*

4. Sell Stuff

Few things feel better than turning clutter into cash. Selling things you do not use anymore not only frees up space but also fuels your travel fund.

The most challenging aspect? Letting go. We all have that one unwanted gift from an almost-stranger that we can't seem to get rid of. It waits on a shelf, a token of politeness, or in a drawer brought out only when its giver reappears. It is less about the thing itself and more about our quiet urge to be kind. It becomes even trickier when the gifts come from people we love. Before you realize it, you are surrounded by items you never use but cannot seem to part with.

When Andy and I moved from the U.S. to Australia, we had to slim our lives down to thirteen 75-pound boxes. Every item went through a ruthless test: Was it replaceable? Did it hold real sentimental value? Was it worth the weight? The rest got sold, donated, or tossed. We felt lighter and more intentional and had extra money to put toward travel.

And it is not only about big-ticket items. I once sold a bag of golf pencils on eBay for $70.

Get rid of some clutter → *$500*

5. Stop Buying New Stuff

It is wild how a closet can be overflowing and yet we still sigh, *"I have nothing to wear."* I have been there, wandering stores without a list, buying things on a whim, only to donate them months later with the tags still on. These days, Andy and I joke about who owns the oldest piece of clothing in our wardrobes. Spoiler: he usually wins.

What changed? We shifted from a "want" mindset to a "need" mindset. Now, before buying something new, we lean on a few simple tricks:

- **The 10/10 Rule:** If it costs under $10, wait 10 minutes before deciding. Anything bigger, wait longer.
- **The 30-Day Rule:** For big-ticket items, sit on it for a month. Chances are that the urge fades.
- **The "Later, Later" Rule:** Ask yourself how you will feel about the purchase in an hour, a day, a month, and a year. If it does not hold up, skip it.

We also follow a **"one in, one out" rule**: if something new comes in, something old must go (ideally sold, not just stuffed in a drawer). The bottom line is that the less money we spend on things we do not really need, the more we have for experiences we will never forget.

Cut $100 of impulse buys per month → $1,200 per year

6. Skip the Gifts

I do not remember who first suggested it, but at some point, Andy and I agreed to stop buying each other gifts and start using that money for experiences instead. We quickly realized those memories lasted far longer than anything we could wrap in paper.

Over time, we extended the idea beyond birthdays. Anniversaries, Christmas, Valentine's Day - all those moments where we might have spent $100 each on gifts got funneled into our Wanderlist fund instead. Sometimes it meant an extra activity in the place we were visiting; sometimes it meant stretching a trip a few days longer. Either way, it always felt like the better trade.

This will not be for everyone. Some people love the ritual of giving (or receiving) gifts, and that joy is real. But if travel is the thing you are both dreaming about, consider reframing a few special occasions each year.

The Lesson: Skip the gifts, swap them for experiences, and turn clutter into memories that last.

⚡ *Swap three $100 gifts each (if a couple) → $600 per year*

7. Use Digital Wallet Round-Ups

Back before digital wallets, Andy and I had a giant coin jar in the corner of our kitchen. Before every trip, we would lug it to the grocery store and feed it into one of those noisy counting machines. The ridiculous clatter of coins always felt like a lottery win, as did walking out with a few hundred extra dollars in travel money. Even the rejected coins were fun souvenirs from past trips that had slipped into the mix.

Today, the jar has gone digital. Many banks and apps enable you to "round up" your purchases to the nearest dollar and funnel the difference into a savings account. When you buy something for $4.75, the stray 25 cents sneaks straight into your travel fund.

It may not sound like much, but those tiny drips add up fast. A grocery run here, some gas there, and suddenly you have got enough for a whale-watching trip on your next getaway, or even a hot-air balloon ride at sunrise.

⚡*Save $35 per month in "change" → $420 per year*

8. Start a Side Hustle

Sometimes the fastest way to build your travel fund is not cutting back; it is earning more. A side hustle does not have to be a second career; it just needs to bring in a little extra for your Wanderlist account.

I have had a handful of side hustles over the years, selling prints, dabbling in stock photography, and, yes, even writing this book. None of them were life-changing on their own, but together they became a steady drip into our travel fund. That drip contributed towards plane tickets, park permits, and the occasional splurge we would not have justified otherwise.

The trick is finding something you do not hate doing after hours, such as dog walking, tutoring, or teaching Pilates. Just be careful not to burn out. A side hustle should add energy and possibility, not leave you too drained to enjoy the adventures you are saving for.

⚡*Do two micro-gigs per month at 125 each → $3,000 per year*

9. **Live a Modest Lifestyle**

This one is not flashy, but it works. The more you keep your everyday life modest, the more room you will have to pour money into travel.

We did not always live this way. Back in Chicago, our garage had two luxury cars, both with hefty monthly payments. When we relocated to Melbourne, we flipped the script. Instead of owning cars, we relied on walking, public transport, and the occasional car-share for weekend getaways. We eventually did buy a car; we paid cash for a basic model and have no regrets.

This does not mean eliminating every expense. At one point, a financial advisor questioned why I paid for an expensive gym membership, and I knew exactly why. It boosted my mental well-being and built a healthy habit that has stuck with me ever since. Some investments in yourself are worth every cent.

The trick is knowing the difference. Every dollar not spent on unnecessary things can take you somewhere amazing.

⚡*Reduce one recurring cost by $100 per month → $1,200 per year*

10. Automate Your Savings

Want to grow your travel fund without even thinking about it? Take the decision-making out of it. Set up an automatic transfer from your everyday account into a separate savings account labeled just for travel. Naming it helps too. It is a lot harder to raid an account called *Epic Safari* to buy a new blender, a pair of sneakers, or takeout sushi. Better yet, keep this account in a high-yield savings account at a different bank than the one you use for daily spending. That extra step makes it harder to dip into on impulse, and your money earns more while it waits.

If your goal is $5,000 in 10 months, set up a system where $500 moves automatically each month into your travel account.

We plan about 18 months ahead, so the money is there when deposits and final payments come due. Save for when you need to pay, not when you plan to go. The trick is to treat travel savings like a bill. Pay yourself first, not with whatever is left over.

Auto-transfer $300 per month → $3,600 per year

11. Automate windfalls

Windfalls are easy to fritter away if you do not give them a job. Tax refunds, work bonuses, or even birthday money can vanish into daily spending unless you lock them in. We have made it a rule: anything unexpected goes straight into the travel account. That way, a tax refund does not just disappear into groceries or gadgets; it funds deposits for our next big trip.

Save a $500 tax refund

12. Check Your Services

Your biggest recurring bills - insurance, phone plans, and utilities - are often the easiest to shrink. We have switched insurers twice and phone plans and utilities more times than I can count, usually shaving $50–$100 off the monthly bill. That is a flight in a few months, in exchange for making a couple of phone calls.

Switch providers to save $60 per month → $720 per year

13. Challenge Yourself to a No-Spend Month

A no-spend month sounds restrictive, but frame it as an experiment (a spending cleanse, if you will), and it can be fun. For 30 days, refrain from purchasing new clothes, dining out, or making impulse purchases. Track what you save and earmark it for travel.

One experiment → $600

Here is an example of how the little changes could stack up:

Scrutinize your spending	$2,400
Cancel subscriptions	$600
Eat at home more	$3,120
Sell stuff	$500
Stop buying new stuff	$1,200
Skip the gifts	$600
Digital wallet round-ups	$420
Start a side hustle	$3,000
Live modestly	$1,200
Automate savings	$3,600
Automate windfalls	$500
Check services	$720
No-spend month	$600
Total Annual Savings	**$18,460**

Everyone's numbers will vary. Maybe you get an annual bonus at work. Maybe you do not have anything to sell (though I strongly doubt that). You may be able to try one of these tactics, or you may want to try them all. The point is that the money for your Wanderlist may already be within reach. A few small, repeatable choices can power entire adventures when you let them compound.

How to Spend Less When You Travel

So far, we have talked about building your travel fund. But saving does not stop once you board the plane. The choices you make on the road can stretch your budget just as much as the ones you make at home.

This is not a book about budget travel; that is not my lane. But over the years, we have picked up a handful of smart strategies that shave costs without sacrificing the experience. These tricks do not just save money; they free up resources so you can say yes to more adventures.

Here are five rules I live by to spend less when I travel, plus a bonus tip I heard once and never forgot.

1. **Consider Shoulder and Off-Season Travel**

    When you travel during shoulder or off-season, you can save a significant amount of money and avoid the worst of the crowds. You will often get the same landscapes and experiences at a fraction of the price, with the bonus of a little more breathing room.

    When we first moved to Australia, we thought we had scored a wonderful bargain on a sailboat charter in the

Whitsundays over Christmas. Only later did we realize why: it was "stinger season." That is the time of year when potentially deadly tiny Irukandji jellyfish drift through the waters, so every swim requires a full-body stinger suit. The gallon jug of vinegar we found in the galley suddenly made a lot of sense.

Or there was the time we booked a beachfront bungalow in the Perhentians during Ramadan at an incredible discount because most locals were not traveling. We were aware it was Ramadan; however, we had not considered how it would affect the availability of services. The ferry town was silent all afternoon, and by the time the first food stalls opened at sunset, that plate of nasi lemak was the best thing we ate the entire trip.

The lesson? Off-season deals can come with quirks. Sometimes it is jellyfish, sometimes it is rain, and sometimes it is shorter opening hours. Do your homework so you know what you are trading. And remember, the trade-offs are not always bad. A little flexibility in timing can turn into big savings and occasionally an even better story.

2. Leverage Loyalty Programs and Sign-Up Bonuses

Loyalty programs are not just about collecting points. Used wisely, they can open doors to flights, hotels, and experiences you might never splurge on with cash.

Airline and hotel programs are the big ones, but do not stop there. Car rental companies, grocery stores, and even retail chains all have loyalty programs that can shave costs off everyday spending and funnel those savings into travel. Search for opportunities everywhere, not just when you book a flight.

Here is a personal example. Andy and I once sat through a Marriott timeshare presentation just to get a stack of points. Combine those with a credit card sign-up bonus, and suddenly we had enough for an entire holiday at the Westin Hapuna in Hawaii, a place we never would have paid cash to stay. The room, the views, the beach - it all felt like luxury we had hacked our way into.

Important: When it comes to credit cards, only play the points game if you can pay off your balance in full each month. Opening new cards can affect your credit score, so treat it as a tool, not free money.

The Takeaway: Loyalty points add up faster than you think, especially when you stack programs. A few sign-ups today could translate into a trip tomorrow.

3. **Master the When-to-Book Game**

Booking early or waiting until the last minute can both save you money; it just depends on your risk tolerance and how much flexibility you are willing to build into your plans.

When we booked our once-in-a-lifetime trip to Antarctica, we locked in our expedition nearly two years in advance and saved about 20%. It gave us peace of mind and guaranteed spots on optional activities like snorkeling and kayaking. But here is the shocker: a few months before departure, we discovered that other ships were offering a 40% discount! That is the trade-off. Book early and you pay for certainty. Book late, and you gamble on availability but might land a decent discount.

We use a similar strategy with flights. Often, we will book a flexible fare months in advance, then keep an eye on reward seats. If they become available a few weeks before, we will switch to those and either get a credit or refund for the original ticket. It takes patience, but the savings add up.

And then there is the overbooked flights hack. Back when I was living in the US, I made a habit of volunteering my seat. As Andy and I settled into our seats on a flight back from the Caribbean, the airline announced they needed 10 volunteers. They offered $1,000 per volunteer, in addition to hotel and meal vouchers. We did not even need to discuss it; both of us grabbed our carry-on luggage and raced off the plane. Another time, when I was commuting weekly for work, I knew Thursday flights were always packed, so I planned around it, turning bumps into a steady stream of travel vouchers.

Whether you are a traveler who thrives on certainty or one who embraces uncertainty, flexibility can pay off in big ways.

Pro Tip: If you have got the wiggle room for last-minute travel, follow tour operators, airlines, and accommodations on social media and sign up for their email newsletters. They often share cancellations or flash deals there first and sometimes at a fraction of the price.

4. **Travel in Groups**

Here is the thing about traveling with others: splitting costs can unlock opportunities that you might not be able to access on your own. Shared cabins, group discounts, or pooling resources can make big adventures suddenly affordable.

One of the first trips Andy and I took as a couple was to the British Virgin Islands. We wanted to see more than just one beach, so we chartered a 50-foot sailboat. With Andy's sailing skills and my ability to follow directions, we invited two other couples, split the costs, and suddenly had a floating home that let us hop from island to island. *This trip may sound bougie, but it worked out to about $400 per person for the entire week (closer to $800 at today's rates).*

Botswana was another case. Most lodges there were way out of our budget until we found a small group camping safari. We experienced the same wildlife and landscapes, just with canvas tents instead of luxury chalets. We spent ten days, made new friends, and created memories we still talk about today.

The bonus? Sharing sunsets on a boat deck or stories around a campfire often becomes just as unforgettable as the destination itself.

5. **Be Intentional with How You Spend Money While Traveling**

Being intentional with your spending is about knowing what matters most to you and putting your money there.

For me, that means splurging on private guides and transport so I can focus on wildlife photography. On safari, that once meant spending three hours parked under a tree where a leopard was resting. Other vehicles arrived and departed; their guides had to keep everyone in the car satisfied. However, having a private guide gave me the freedom to stay, and that kind of flexibility is worth every cent to me.

But intention is not just about big-ticket choices; it is also about the small daily ones that quietly add up. Last year, we stayed at a hotel where coffee was eight dollars a cup. During our stay, we drank four cups of coffee a day for five days, and the quality was disappointing. Since then, we started traveling with a small French press. It paid for itself in three mornings, and the coffee has been better ever since.

What do I skip? Souvenirs. Well, mostly. On a recent trip to Alaska, I purposely did not pack a hoodie so I could buy one as a keepsake. I ended up buying two, but only after thinking about it for three days (*Later, Later Rule*) and making space by donating a few old ones when I got home (*One in, One out Rule*). Now, instead of clutter, I have memories that I can wear.

Bonus Tip: Rent Your Home While You Are Away

Why let your place sit empty while you are off having a European summer when it could be quietly paying for part of your trip? We have not done this personally, but friends of ours rented their home for just two weeks, and the income basically covered their flights and meals.

Of course, there are a few basics to check first. Make sure short-term rentals are allowed in your area, tuck away or lock up anything personal, and use a platform like Airbnb or VRBO to handle bookings, payments, and insurance. Once that is sorted, the process could be surprisingly easy.

The best part? A single rental stint could cover your flights, a couple of hotel nights, or even that splurge activity you were not sure you could justify. Your house works for you while you work through your Wanderlist.

In Summary

The strategies in this chapter are about making your money work for your adventures. Small changes, repeated over time, add up; that is the compound effect in action. Whether it is cooking at home, ditching unused subscriptions, or automating your savings, every choice moves you closer to your next trip. The goal is not sacrifice; it is being intentional so your resources flow toward what matters most. With these habits in place, your travel dreams stop being "someday" and start becoming real.

Now it is your turn. The next activity will help you identify these money-saving habits, so you can start a travel fund and ensure you have the cash when your dream trips come calling.

ACTIVITY

Develop a Savings Plan

When it comes to saving for travel, it is not always about making drastic sacrifices; it is about being mindful of your daily habits and making small adjustments that can add up in a big way. This activity will help you take a close look at your current spending patterns, identify areas where you can cut back, and create new systems to ensure your savings go straight to your travel fund.

This is the activity most people want to skip, but hang in there. Think of it less like crunching numbers and more like building your personal *adventure fund*. Start today, even if it is small. Without a plan, your Wanderlist stays an idea, and with one, it becomes possible.

---

1. **Calculate how much you need by when**

   To figure out how much you need to save, you need to know two things: the total cost and when each payment is due. Timing can entirely change what feels possible.

Say you want to take a $3,000 trip in six months, and the full amount is due three months before departure. You would need to save the whole $3,000 in three months, or $1,000 per month.

Now flip it. If you can save $1,000 per month, you might prefer to put that toward a bigger dream trip that costs $10,000. Book it for 18 months from now, with a deposit due at 12 months and the balance due 90 days before departure. You would need to save about $667 per month to have the full $10,000 by the balance deadline.

The Point: timelines change everything. A $10,000 trip sounds impossible until you spread it over 18 or even 24 months; then it feels like a manageable monthly bill. A $3,000 trip is easy if you plan a year out, but if you want to go this summer, you will need to hustle.

So ask yourself: **how much do you need, and by when**? Do not worry if you do not have exact numbers yet. Choosing a rough estimate and practicing the exercise is more effective than delaying until you have precise details.

2. **Identify opportunities to save (and make a commitment)**

Now that you know how much you need and when, the next step is to figure out *where the money will come from*. Revisit the tactics from earlier in this chapter and choose a few that make sense for you.

For each one, write down four things:

- **Goal:** What specific change will you make?
- **Savings**: How much will it realistically save you?
- **System**: What will keep you on track?
- **Outcome**: What does that add up to over time?

For example:

- **Goal**: I will stop buying take-away lunches.
- **Savings**: $50 per week.
- **System**: Meal-prep every Sunday for the week ahead.
- **Outcome**: $2,000 saved in 10 months.

If this is your first time trying it, start simple. Pick a few easy wins, like

- Cut or downgrade three subscriptions you barely use.
- Sell nine items in your home this month.
- Identify seven ways to trim daily spending (coffee runs, impulse buys, delivery fees).
- Try a 30-day "no-spend" challenge for non-essentials.

The Point: small, consistent choices compound fast. Every $20 you free up each week is another $1,000 toward your next trip.

3. **Automate your savings**

Now it is time to make your plan foolproof. The goal here is to take the willpower out of saving so it happens in the background. Once you have gotten your number, automate it:

- Open a separate, high-interest account. Give it a name that makes you smile, like *Patagonia Hiking Adventure* or *California Road Trip - 2026.*
- Set up automatic transfers for the exact amount you need, timed with your paycheck. Better yet, split it into smaller, more frequent transfers so you barely notice it leaving your account.

If the numbers still look intimidating, do not panic. You have got levers you can pull:

- Add another savings tactic (or three or four!).
- Cut a little deeper into discretionary spending.
- Trim the cost of the trip.
- Or simply push the trip out a few months to give yourself more time.

Once you have completed this activity, you will have a concrete plan that tells you exactly what behavioral changes you need to make to reach your savings goal.

Instead of relying on vague wishes, you will have a dependable system.

The trick is to treat savings like a bill you always pay, not whatever is left at the end of the month. This will ensure that you have the funds when deposits or final payments are due. Your numbers will shift as life changes, and that is normal. What matters is that you have built a system.

Recap of Step 5 - Overcoming Financial Obstacles

Money does not have to be the barrier that keeps your trips as "someday." With the right habits, it becomes the fuel that makes them possible.

In Step 5, you:

- Explored practical strategies to adjust your daily spending and free up cash for travel.
- Learned how budgeting, auditing expenses, and automating savings can keep you on track.
- Discovered how small, consistent choices add up over time, turning coffee money and spare change into flights, safaris, and road trips.

With these tools in place, you can fund your Wanderlist without debt or guilt, knowing your money is working toward the adventures that matter most.

Savings is your energy.
Every dollar stored powers the road to your next adventure.

Wanderlist Journey

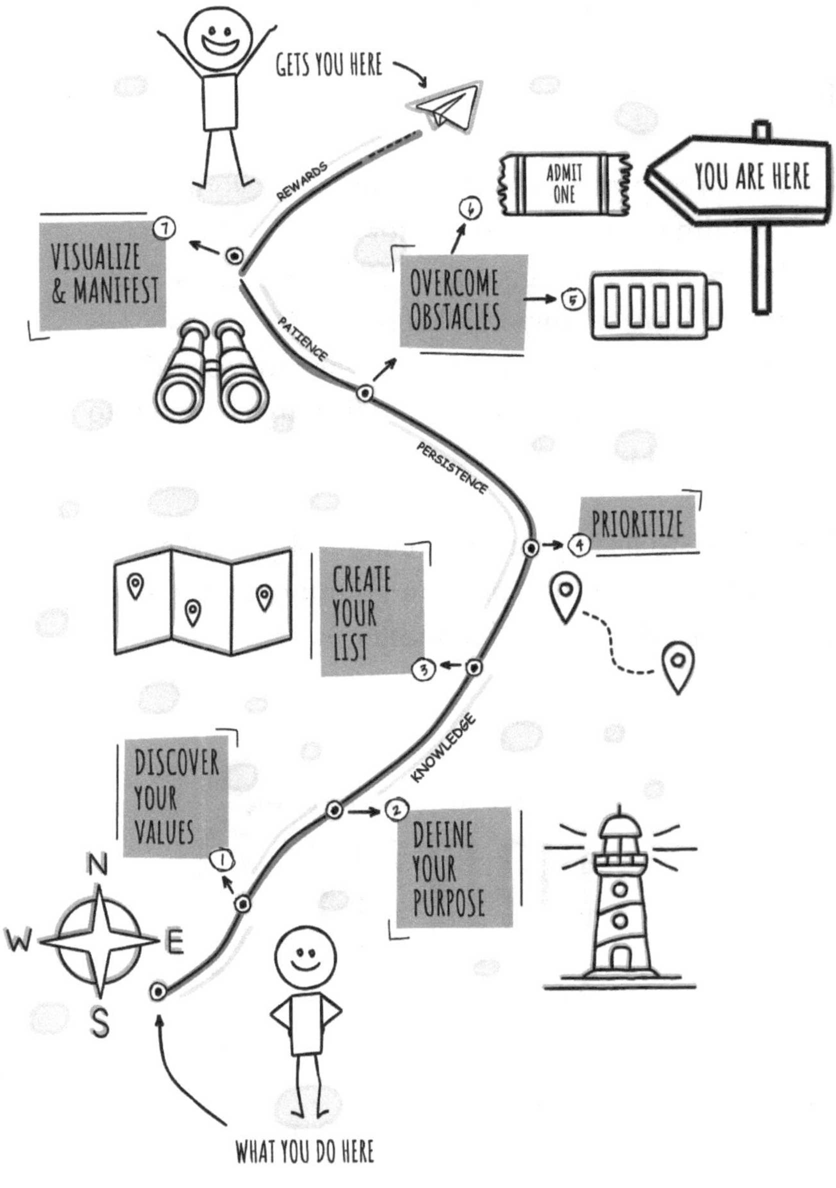

Step 6

HACKING YOUR ANNUAL LEAVE

When I lived in the U.S., I had three weeks of annual leave to work with. Each year, Andy and I would sit down with a calendar, mark the public holidays, and plan how to stretch those 15 days into the longest breaks possible. It became something of a running joke at work, and once, a performance review even described me as *"a role model for work-life balance."*

The truth is, most of us do not have endless time off, and some people don't have paid leave at all. But wherever you are starting from, a little strategy goes a long way. By mixing public holidays, weekends, and the occasional red-eye, you can squeeze a surprising amount of adventure out of even the smallest window of time.

In this step, we will look at how to understand your employer's leave policies, make the most of long weekends, piggyback travel onto work trips, and use tricks like overnight flights and mini escapes to stretch your time.

If your Wanderlist is the map and your savings is the fuel, then annual leave is the toolbox that helps you travel more.

Understand Annual Leave Policies

Before you can stretch your annual leave, you need to know the rules of the game. Every company handles time off differently. Some let days roll over, some are strict "use it or lose it," and some even let you buy extra days or take unpaid leave to extend a trip.

It is crucial to review the details so you do not accidentally leave vacation on the table. When I was leading global teams, I always checked in with people to ensure they knew their local rules and used everything they were entitled to. No member of my team was going to lose a day off on my watch.

And here is a personal lesson: before I moved to Australia, I had never traveled here because the flight basically takes two days, blowing through a big chunk of my limited U.S. vacation time. Looking back, I should have asked about unpaid leave to make it possible. Worst-case, they could have said no.

The same applies to you: know your options, know the deadlines, and do not be afraid to ask. Those days are yours. Make them work as hard for you as possible.

Identify Public Holidays and Weekends

One of the easiest hacks to stretch your leave is by piggybacking on public holidays. Align your annual leave days with weekends and public holidays, and suddenly your two weeks of leave can feel like three.

During my first year in Australia, it felt like I won the public holiday lottery. Good Friday, Easter Monday, and ANZAC Day all lined up, which meant I could take just 8 days of annual leave and turn it into a 16-day trip. Andy and I flew to Auckland, picked up a campervan, and spent two weeks winding our way through New Zealand's South Island. The only downside? Half of Australia and New Zealand had the same idea. Public holidays are excellent for maximizing time off, but they also come with higher prices and bigger crowds.

Since then, plotting public holidays and weaving them into our plans has become an annual tradition. A quick Google search for "annual leave hacks + [your city] + [year]" will usually surface local guides with the best dates. Or, if you want something more tailored, try asking an AI tool to map out your leave around your preferences. Just remember, like all tools, the answers are only as good as the data they are drawing from.

Add-On to a Work Trip

Mixing business with leisure is one of the smartest ways to stretch your travel time. If flights are already covered by work, adding a few extra days can turn a routine trip into a mini adventure, often without using much additional leave.

I learned this trick in graduate school, when I submitted a proposal to speak at a conference in Greece because, well, it was in Greece. To my surprise, it was accepted. The conference covered part of the travel expenses, and by booking with points, I even scored a 48-hour layover in Barcelona on the way home. Not bad for an academic assignment.

Most work trips are not this glamorous and are usually confined to airports, hotels, and conference rooms in mundane locations. But with a little foresight, I have been able to turn them into adventures. A client meeting in Las Vegas became the perfect excuse to detour to Antelope Canyon. A Perth workshop gave me the chance to spend a weekend snorkeling with sea lions. And a few days in Brisbane stretched into a long weekend on Lady Elliot Island, where I traded meetings for manta rays.

There are risks, though. I once booked a jaguar expedition in the Pantanal to follow a work trip to Brazil, only to have the business part cancelled two weeks before departure. Fortunately, travel insurance cushioned the blow, and we managed to visit this destination a few years later.

The takeaway? Understand your employer's policies, buy travel insurance, and whenever work takes you somewhere, ask yourself, "What can I add on?"

Embrace Overnight Flights

Overnight flights can be a game-changer when it comes to stretching your annual leave. Think of it as teleporting to your destination while you sleep. Flying out after your workday ends and landing just in time to start a new day somewhere new effectively adds whole days to your vacation without depleting your leave. You save on accommodation for the night and wake up ready to explore. With a little planning, red eyes can turn wasted hours into bonus adventure time.

That said, this tactic is not for every trip. In my twenties and thirties, I could do an overnight flight both ways and sometimes land straight into a workday. These days, I am more likely to take a morning departure. The key takeaway is that overnight flights serve as a valuable tool in your travel toolkit; use them when you want to maximize days on vacation and skip them when the itinerary demands a slower pace.

Take Mini Escapes

Not every adventure has to be a long-haul flight or a once-in-a-lifetime splurge. Mini escapes, a weekend road trip, a quick hop to the mountains or coast, or even a single overnight somewhere new can give you the reset you need without draining your leave balance. They are easier to plan, lighter on the wallet, and often just as memorable as the big-ticket journeys.

The trick is to make them intentional. Go back to your values and purpose, even for short trips, so they feel like part of your Wanderlist rather than just random getaways.

When we lived in Texas, we spent a weekend photographing roseate spoonbills (big pink birds) on the coast. It cost next to nothing, ticked all the boxes of nature and adventure that matter to me, and delivered the same sense of wonder I usually chase on bigger trips. Those small escapes kept me fueled between the headline adventures and reminded me that meaning is not measured in dollars or miles.

In Summary

By mastering the art of annual leave hacking, you can unlock more time for travel without burning through all your days off. From knowing your employer's policies and making the most of public holidays to stretching work trips and sneaking in mini escapes, these tactics help you squeeze more adventure out of the same calendar. The goal is to travel smarter, so every hard-earned day off takes you further.

Let me be crystal clear (ok, blunt): avoid scheduling your trips around what *might* happen at work. Work will not plan around you, so do not give it power over your plans.

I cannot tell you how many times I have heard, *"I was going to book something over <insert holiday here>, but there is <insert work thing here> scheduled then."* Guess what? Work dates shift. Projects move. The only thing you can count on is that work will always want more of you. The real question is: do you want to live to work, or work to live?

Now it is your turn. The next activity will help you map out your annual leave days and spot the hidden windows where a little planning turns into a lot more time away.

ACTIVITY

Plan your Annual Leave

Maximizing annual leave is not about working less; it is about planning smarter. By being strategic with your days off, you can stretch a limited leave budget into long adventures, quick escapes, and everything in between. This activity will help you map out your leave, so you get the most travel time possible.

Do not delay. The sooner you know what time you are working with, the sooner you can be on your way.

---

1. **Review your leave balance**

   Start with the basics: how many days do you have? Check your employer's policies for:

   - Total available annual leave days.
   - Blackout dates or restrictions on when you can take leave.
   - Options to buy extra leave, compress your work week, or take unpaid days.

This gives you a clear picture of what is possible before you start plotting.

2. **Research public holidays**

Next, look at public holidays and how they align with weekends. These are the golden tickets that let you travel more frequently or for longer durations.

Do not forget "bonus" days too, like the day after Thanksgiving in the U.S. or office-wide shutdowns between Christmas and New Year's. Note them all down so you can start spotting potential windows for longer trips.

3. **Build your strategy**

Now it is time to put the pieces together. Think about the following:

- Do you prefer one or two longer adventures, or multiple short getaways?
- Are there certain months you need to plan around (e.g., school holidays, peak seasons, family events)?
- Can you pair work trips, overnight flights, or mini escapes with your leave to stretch it even further?

I like using AI (e.g., ChatGPT, Microsoft Copilot, and Google Gemini) as a starting point. Here is a sample prompt:

Act as a travel planner and optimization expert.
I have 15 days of annual leave in 2026.
I also have the following public holidays: January 1, May 25, July 3, September 7, November 26, and December 25.
My employer provides the week of July 4 and the days between Christmas and New Year's as additional paid time off.
I want to maximize my total time off by planning around weekends and public holidays.
Please:

1. Suggest the best dates to take my leave in 2026.
2. Include two trips of about 10–12 days each, plus some shorter breaks.
3. Ensure one longer trip happens in **April**.
4. Explain your reasoning briefly so I can adjust the plan if needed.

Once you have completed this activity, you will have a strategy that shows not just how many days you are taking, but how much time you are really getting. A little foresight now means more adventure later.

Recap of Step 6 – Hacking Your Annual Leave

Time does not have to be the barrier that keeps your adventures out of reach. With smart planning, your annual leave becomes the key to unlocking more travel than you thought possible.

In Step 6, you:

- Explored how to understand your employer's leave policies and make the most of public holidays.
- Learned how to extend trips by adding leisure days to work travel and embracing mini escapes.
- Discovered strategies, from overnight flights to AI tools, to stretch limited days off into meaningful adventures.

With these tactics in place, you can turn even a modest leave balance into a year full of purposeful journeys, making your Wanderlist a reality one trip at a time.

Time is your ticket. Use it wisely, and every day off goes further.

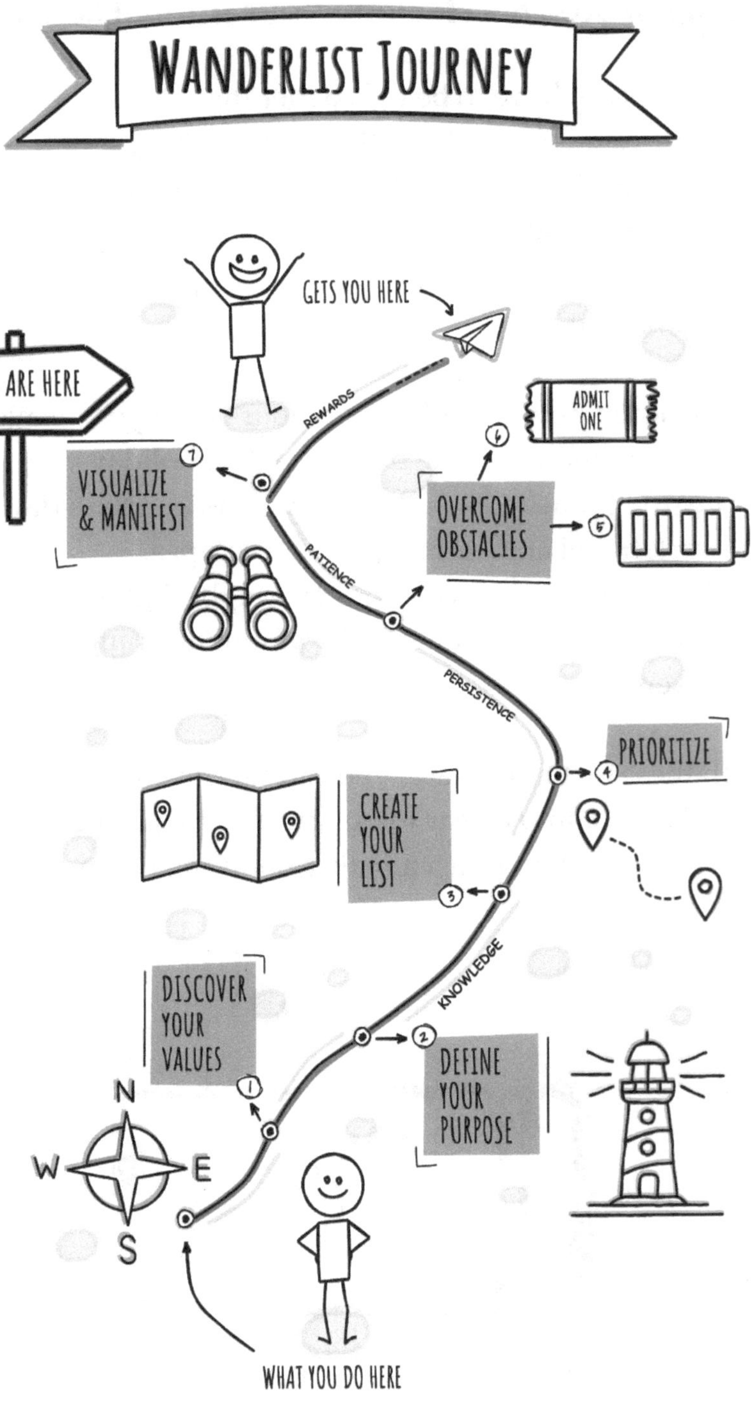

WANDERLIST JOURNEY
GETS YOU HERE
YOU ARE HERE
REWARDS
ADMIT ONE
6
7
VISUALIZE & MANIFEST
OVERCOME OBSTACLES
5
PATIENCE
PERSISTENCE
PRIORITIZE
4
CREATE YOUR LIST
3
KNOWLEDGE
DISCOVER YOUR VALUES
1
2
DEFINE YOUR PURPOSE
N
W
E
S
WHAT YOU DO HERE

Step 7

VISUALIZING & MANIFESTING SUCCESS

Studies show that simply having a trip booked, or even just something to look forward to, gives your happiness a measurable boost. If that is true, then my home office might be the happiest place on earth.

In the corner stands a messy whiteboard, covered in a 36-month grid. Green sticky notes mark the trips already locked in. Yellow stickies are "seriously considering." The pink ones are the backlog, ideas waiting their turn. Some even have little drawings: a puffin here, a bear there. Nearby, a perpetual year dry erase calendar is filled with public holidays and upcoming adventures for the current year. By visualizing it, I can see not just individual trips but how the next few years of travel could unfold. I also have digital versions of all these materials but seeing them in person is powerful.

If your values serve as the compass, your purpose acts as the lighthouse, and your savings provide the fuel, then visualization functions like binoculars; it brings your future adventures into sharper focus. This chapter is about using visualization and reflection to make your Wanderlist feel real, while leaving room for it to evolve as your life and priorities change.

Manifest Your Wanderlist

Visualization is powerful because it helps you see where you want to go. Manifestation takes it one step further. It is about pairing those visions with belief and deliberate action.

Manifestation is not magic; you cannot just imagine penguins and wake up on the ice in Antarctica. But when you clearly define what you want, believe it is possible, and start taking aligned steps, you create momentum that pulls you closer to your dream trip.

Think about the systems you have already built in the earlier steps:

- You know your values and purpose.
- You have created and prioritized your Wanderlist.
- You have built strategies for time and money.

Those tools are the action side of manifestation. The visualization piece, like seeing yourself on a ship in Antarctica or writing a postcard from your future self, is what keeps your motivation alive long enough to follow through.

In short: visualization is the picture. Manifestation is the follow-through. Together, they turn "someday" trips into real experiences.

Evolve Your Wanderlist Over Time

When I was younger and had less time off, my Wanderlist leaned heavily on shorter, "check the box" trips, long weekends in Europe, and quick getaways squeezed into the margins of work. These days, I have shifted toward longer trips. Partly because I finally have the time, but also because they save money: one long-haul flight in and out instead of several shorter ones scattered through the year.

I have also realized that I would rather save for big, impactful experiences than scatter my budget across more frequent, average ones. Snorkeling with beluga whales, walking with polar bears, or photographing puffins may take longer to plan and save for, but they stick with me in a way no whirlwind city breaks ever did.

Reflect on Your Experiences

Travel has also taught me a lot about myself, not just where I want to go, but how I want to live. I am happiest keeping life simple: driving an eight-year-old car, skipping fashion trends, and putting my money toward travel instead. Every time I reflect on a trip, I am reminded that what stays with me is not the stuff I skipped spending money on at home, but the moments I said yes to, like descending into an ice cave in Aoraki/Mt. Cook in New Zealand or trekking with fossa researchers in Madagascar. And yes, fossa are real and not just fictional creatures from the movies.

Those reflections have shaped my Wanderlist into something much deeper than a list of places. It has become a filter for how I live my life, a reminder that experiences matter far more than things.

In Summary

Visualization is what turns your Wanderlist from a list of "somedays" into something you can see taking shape. By mapping it out, sketching it, or even doodling puffins and bears on a whiteboard, you give your dreams a place to live and a way to pull you forward. The clearer the picture, the more motivated you will be to make it real.

Now it is your turn. The next activity will help you bring your future travels into focus with Postcards from the Future, a simple exercise to picture your adventures as if they have already happened.

ACTIVITY

Visualizing Success

Now it is time to bring your Wanderlist to life. You have set your compass, found your lighthouse, mapped your pins, and planned around money and time. This exercise is about seeing it all play out and giving yourself a glimpse of the future you are working toward. And all you need is a blank piece of paper.

Do this now. Do not overthink it or worry about being "artistic." Stick figures and scribbles are fine. What matters is capturing the feeling.

---

1. **Picture the scene**

   Close your eyes and imagine yourself on a future trip. Maybe it is one year from now, maybe twenty. Where are you? What are you seeing, tasting, hearing, and feeling?

2. **Draw your postcard**

   Using a blank piece of paper, on one side, sketch or paste an image (or a few images) that captures that trip. This is not an art competition. It does not have to be pretty: just personal.

3. **Write the message**

   On the other side, write a short note to your present self. Tell yourself where you are, what you just experienced, and why it matters. Sign it with a future date, as if it has really been mailed back in time.

4. **Keep it visible**

   Keep your postcard somewhere visible, such as your refrigerator, desk, or mirror. Let it remind you that this is not just a dream; it is a destination waiting its turn.

Once you have completed this activity, you will have a simple, tangible vision of what you are working toward. It is not art homework. It is fuel for motivation, proof that your future trips are worth the effort today.

Stick it somewhere you will see it often, and let it be your quiet cheerleader every time you are tempted to drift off course.

Recap of Step 7 – Visualizing & Manifesting Success

Visualization is the bridge between dreaming and doing. When you picture your future travels clearly, you provide yourself both the motivation and the direction to make them happen.

In Step 7, you:

- Learned how visualization and manifestation can sharpen your Wanderlist, turning abstract ideas into concrete goals you can act on.
- Explored how to evolve your list over time, adapting it as your values, priorities, and circumstances shift.
- Discovered the power of reflection, using each trip not just as a memory, but as a guidepost for what comes next.

With these tools, your Wanderlist becomes more than a plan. It becomes a living story, pulling you forward, one adventure at a time.

Visualization is your binoculars.
It brings distant dreams into clear view.

It is time to start your Wanderlist Blueprint: Dream big. Plan smart. Travel more.

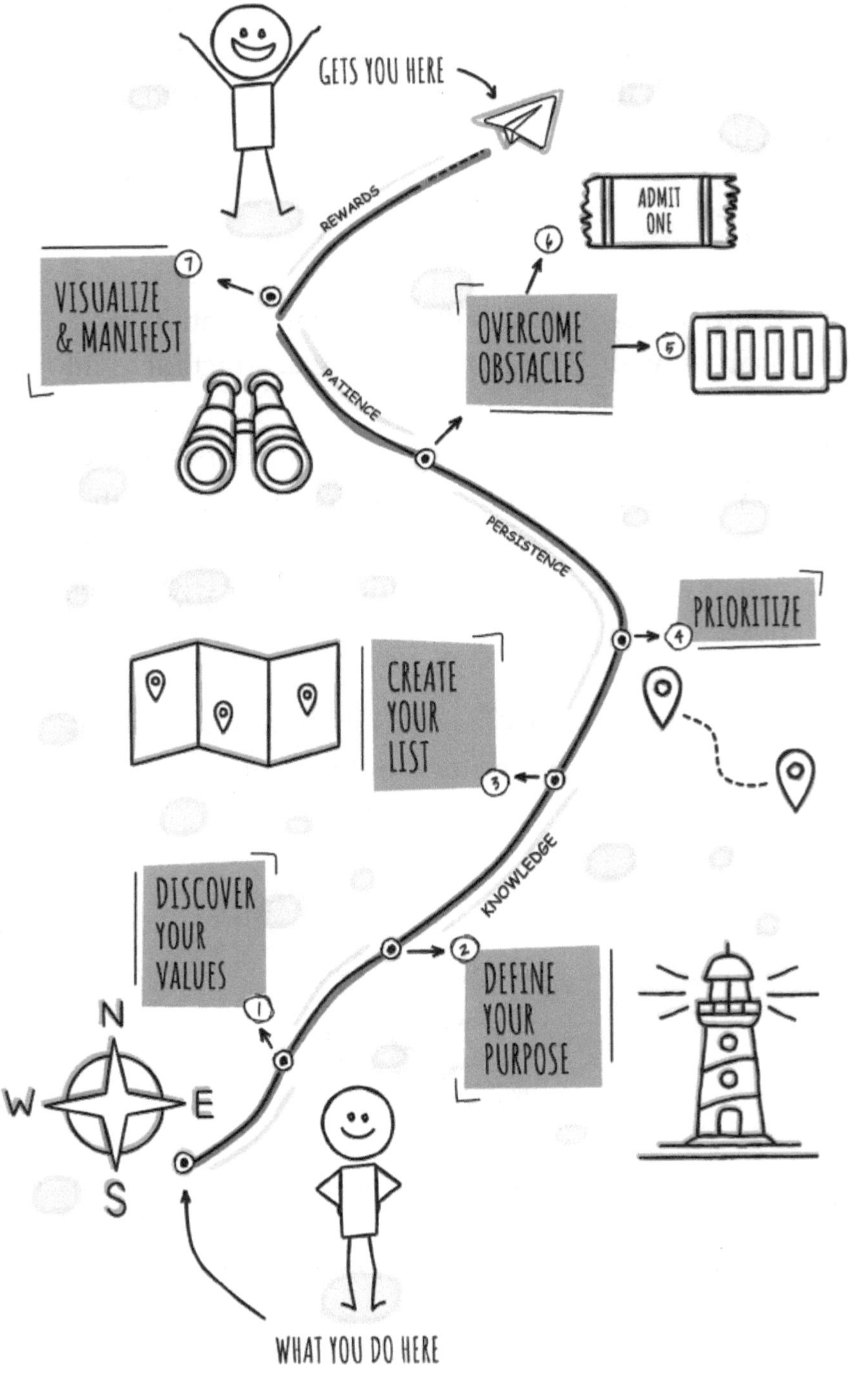

APPENDIX

WANDERLIST BLUEPRINT: QUICK REFERENCE GUIDE

This is your quick reference guide to the Wanderlist Blueprint: the seven steps that will take you from dreaming to doing.

Use these checklists and worksheets as a starting point. For printable, reusable versions (plus bonus tools), download the free Wanderlist Toolkit.

https://bit.ly/wanderlistkit

Discover Your Travel Values

Values are your **compass**. They keep your Wanderlist aligned with what matters most.

At a Glance

- Revisit your list of core values.
- Highlight the ones that shape your travel decisions.
- Keep your top 3 front of mind when reviewing your Wanderlist or choosing trips.

Quick Note

My travel values are

1. ____

2. ____

3. ____

💡 If you do not know your travel values, you risk spending time and money on trips that leave you empty. Your values are not just ideals; they are filters that turn a long list of destinations into the right list for you.

Define Your Travel Purpose

Your purpose is the **lighthouse** guiding your Wanderlist. It keeps you moving toward trips that reflect who you are becoming, not just where you have been.

At a Glance

- Write a short statement of why travel matters to you.
- Keep it personal, not generic. Your purpose should feel like it belongs only to you.
- Use this purpose statement (together with your values) as a filter when deciding what deserves a place on your Wanderlist.

Quick Note

My travel purpose is

If you do not define your purpose, you risk chasing someone else's idea of adventure. Once you do, every trip becomes more than a getaway; it becomes a step toward the life you want to live.

Create Your Wanderlist

Your Wanderlist is a **map** of all the places, adventures, and experiences you dream of, even if they feel out of reach.

At a Glance

- Brainstorm freely. Write down everything that excites you.
- Do not filter or edit yet. This is about imagination, not limits.
- Check each idea against your **purpose and values**. If they do not align, you may need to revisit earlier steps.

Quick Note

I notice the following themes when I review my Wanderlist

My wildcard idea (the one that surprised me most) is

Themes show what consistently matters to you. Wildcards remind you to leave space for surprise, because sometimes the unexpected trips become the most memorable.

Prioritize your Wanderlist

Your priorities are your **route**, the path that takes you from a world of possibilities to the next adventure on your horizon.

At a Glance

- Pick the prioritization methods that make the most sense to you.
- Treat the methods as a starting point, not a final verdict.
- Do not panic if something lands in a place you did not expect. You can always adjust.

Quick Note

My must-do list includes

My aspirational dream trips are

Prioritizing is not about shrinking your dreams; it is about picking the right timing. Say "yes" to what fits now, while keeping the long-horizon adventures alive.

Overcome Financial Obstacles

Savings are your stored **energy**. Every dollar set aside adds power to carry you further along the road to your next adventure.

At a Glance

- There are many ways to save money *for* travel and to save money *while* traveling.
- It is not about depriving yourself of all joy; it is about making small changes that compound into results.

Quick Note

I want to save $________ by __________ .
(amount) (date)

I will do this by

____

____

One giant expense does not block big adventures; hundreds of small, intentional choices unlock them. Do not think of it as what you are giving up. Think about it as what you are choosing instead.

Hack Your Annual Leave

Time is your **ticket**. How you use it determines how far your Wanderlist can take you.

At a Glance

- Figure out how much leave you will need for the trips you are prioritizing.
- Identify the best time to take annual leave, aligning with seasons, events, or life stages.
- Build a multi-year plan so you can see the bigger picture, not just the next holiday.

Quick Note

Unfinished business I need to verify (e.g., unpaid leave, flexible schedules, carryover days)

____

Trips or milestones I will put on the calendar now

____

💡 When you plan your leave with intention, you stop squeezing travel into the gaps of life and start shaping life around the adventures you want.

Visualize and Manifest Success

Visualization acts as your **binoculars**, helping to bring distant dreams into sharper focus so that you can take the necessary steps to make them a reality.

At a Glance

- Picture your future trips in detail: sights, sounds, and feelings.
- Keep reminders visible: countdowns, images, and vision boards.
- Pair every vision with one small action you can take now to move it closer.

Quick Note

The details of my trip that I saw were

The small actions I will take to advance this vision are

Visualization without action is just daydreaming. When you pair imagination with intentional steps, you turn your Wanderlist into lived experience.

Your support means the world to me. If this book inspired you, please consider leaving a review, as it will help others discover *Wanderlist Blueprint*.

For updates, behind-the-scenes stories, and new adventures, visit sharingthe.world and subscribe to my newsletter. I would love to stay connected.

ABOUT THE AUTHOR

Jennifer Martin has spent her life balancing two passions: shaping experiences through design and seeking them through travel and photography.

In her professional life, she built a career in design and innovation, helping organizations solve complex challenges with creative frameworks. Outside of work, she applied those same principles to her passion for travel, rethinking how she planned, budgeted, and prioritized to create a system that allowed her to explore all seven continents twice while maintaining a full-time career. That system became the backbone of *Wanderlist Blueprint.*

Her photography has been featured in exhibitions, conservation projects, and citizen science initiatives, yet her proudest moments are not measured in awards or accolades, but in the words, *"I booked that trip because of your photo."*

Originally from the United States, Jennifer now lives in coastal Victoria, Australia, where kangaroos are her neighbors and the next adventure is always on the horizon.